NCAA BASKETBALL OFFENSE

Plays 2017-2018

NCAA Basketball offensePlays 2017-2018

NCAA Basketball offense — Plays 2017-2018

Title: NCAA Basketball offense: Plays 2017-2018
Acoach MM
Edited by: Acoachmm
Colection: Pure basketball plays 5
First edition: March 2018
Only for coaches
facebook: www.facebook.com/acoachmm
Twitter: @acoachmmbasket

NCAA Basketball offense   Plays 2017-2018

NCAA Basketball offense

Alabama Crimson Tide	8
Arizona Wildcats	15
Arizona State Sun Devils	21
Baylor Bears	28
Cincinnati Bearcats	34
Duke Blue Devils	40
Florida Gators	47
Florida State Seminoles	52
Gonzaga Bulldogs	59
Kansas Jayhawks	66
Kentucky Wildcats	72
Miami Hurricanes	78
Michigan State Spartans	84
Minnesota Golden Gophers	91
North Carolina Tar Heels	98
Notre Dame Fighting Irish	105
Oklahoma Sooners	111
Purdue Boilermakers	117
Seton Hall Pirates	124
TCU Horned Frogs	130
Tennesee Volunteers	136
Texas A&M Aggies	142
Texas Longhorns	148
Texas Tech Red Raiders	154
Ucla Bruins	160
Villanova Wildcats	167
Virginia Cavaliers	173
West Virginia Mountaineers	179
Wichita State Shockers	186
Xavier Musketeers	192
Index plays	198

NCAA Basketball offense   Plays 2017-2018

NCAA Basketball offense   Plays 2017-2018

Keys

NCAA Basketball offense — Plays 2017-2018

SEC Conference

ALABAMA CRIMSON TIDE

Roster

#	Name	Position	Role
0	Donta Hall	Center	Starter
1	Riley Norris	Small Forward	
2	Collin Sexton	Point Guard	Starter Star
3	Alex Reese	Power Forward	
4	Daniel Giddens	Center	
5	Avery Johnson Jr.	Point Guard	
10	Herbert Jones		
11	Tevin Mack		
12	Dazon Ingram	Small Forward	Starter
22	Ar´mond Davis		
23	John Petty	Shooting Guard	Starter
24	Lawson Schaffer		
25	Braxton Key	Small Forward	Starter
30	Galin Smith	Power Forward	
33	Landon Fuller		

Head coach	Avery Johnson
Asociate H. coach	John Pelphrey
Assistant coach	Antoine Pettway
Assistant coach	Yasir Rosemond

NCAA Basketball offense — Plays 2017-2018

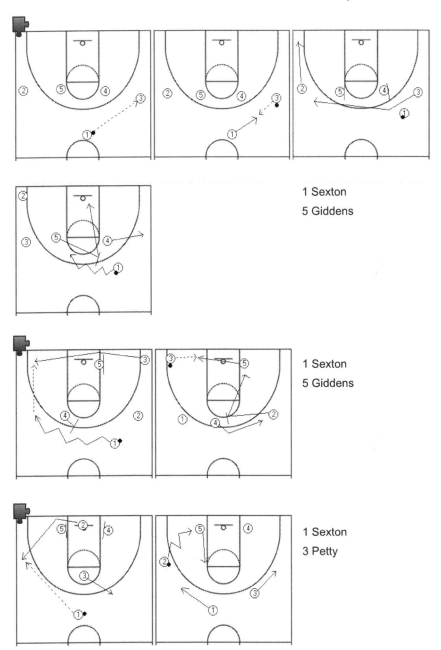

1 Sexton
5 Giddens

1 Sexton
5 Giddens

1 Sexton
3 Petty

Alabama Crimson Tide

NCAA Basketball offense — Plays 2017-2018

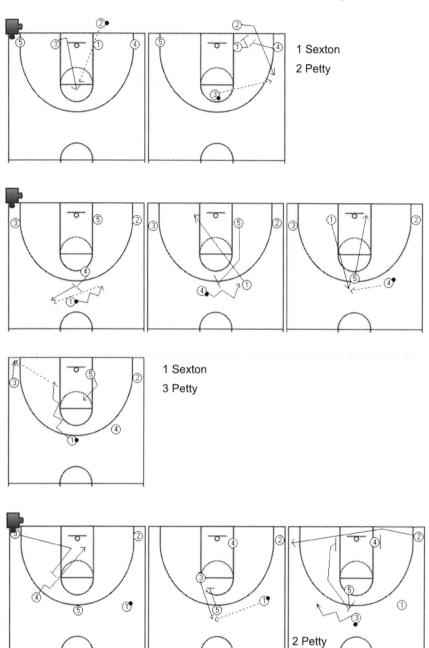

1 Sexton
2 Petty

1 Sexton
3 Petty

2 Petty

Alabama Crimson Tide

NCAA Basketball offense — Plays 2017-2018

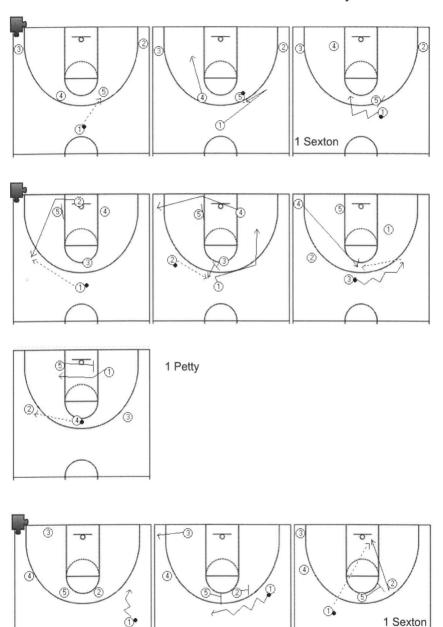

1 Sexton

1 Petty

1 Sexton
2 Petty

Alabama Crimson Tide

NCAA Basketball offense   Plays 2017-2018

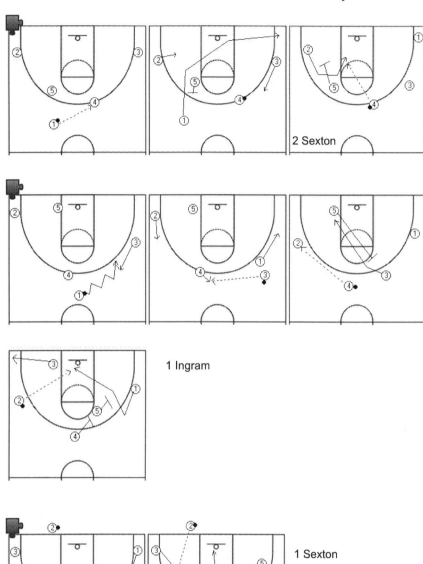

2 Sexton

1 Ingram

1 Sexton

Alabama Crimson Tide

NCAA Basketball offense — Plays 2017-2018

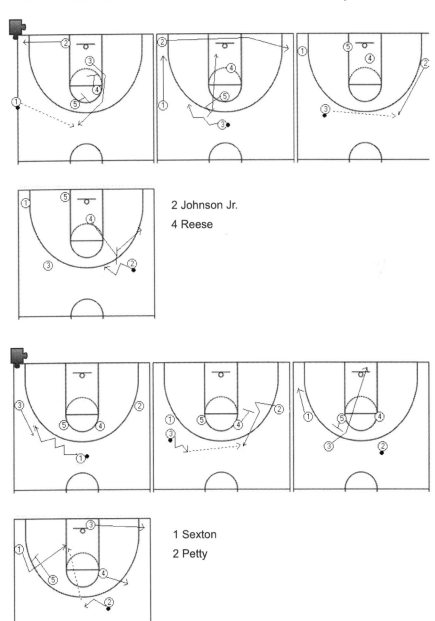

2 Johnson Jr.
4 Reese

1 Sexton
2 Petty

Alabama Crimson Tide   13

NCAA Basketball offense   Plays 2017-2018

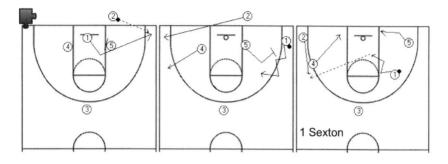

1 Sexton

Alabama Crimson Tide

NCAA Basketball offense Plays 2017-2018

PAC - 12

ARIZONA WILDCATS

Roster

#	Name	Position	Role
0	Parker Jackson-Cartwright	Point Guard	Starter
1	Rawle Alkins	Shooting Guard	Starter
3	Dylan Smith		
4	Chase Jeter	Center	
5	Brandon Randolph	Small Forward	
11	Ira Lee	Power Forward	
13	DeAndre Ayton	Center	Starter Star
14	Dusan Ristic	Center	Starter
20	Talbott Denny		
23	Alex Barcello	Point Guard	
24	Emmanuel Akot	Small Forward	
25	Keanu Pinder	Power Forward	
35	Allonzo Trier	Shooting Guard	Starter Scorer
50	Tyler Trillo		
52	Kory Jones		
54	Matt Weyand		
55	Jake Desjardins		

Head coach   Sean Miller
Asociate H. coach   Lorenzo Romar
Assistant coach   Mark Phelps

15

NCAA Basketball offense   Plays 2017-2018

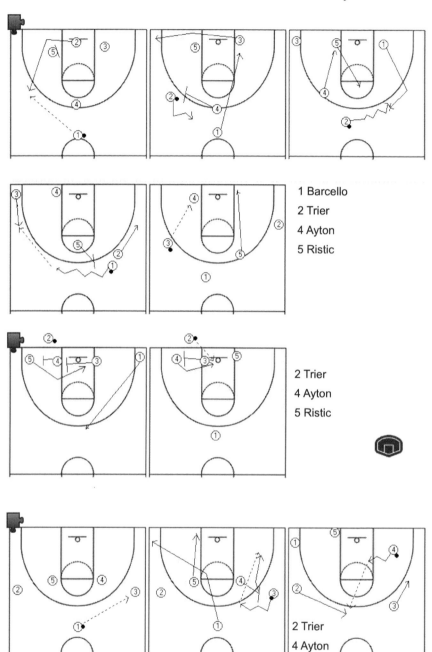

1 Barcello
2 Trier
4 Ayton
5 Ristic

2 Trier
4 Ayton
5 Ristic

2 Trier
4 Ayton

Arizona Wildcats   16

NCAA Basketball offense — Plays 2017-2018

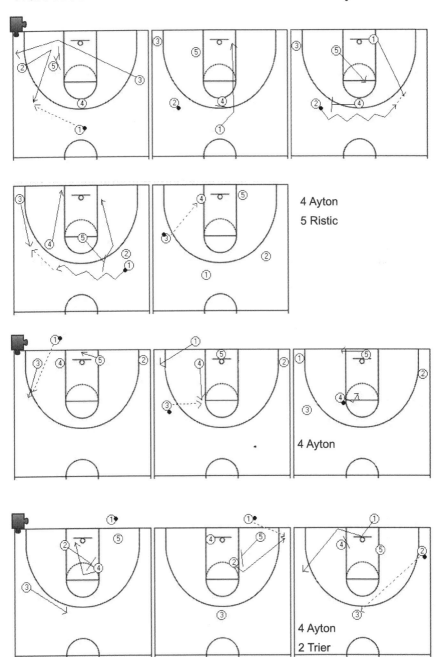

4 Ayton
5 Ristic

4 Ayton

4 Ayton
2 Trier

Arizona Wildcats

NCAA Basketball offense — Plays 2017-2018

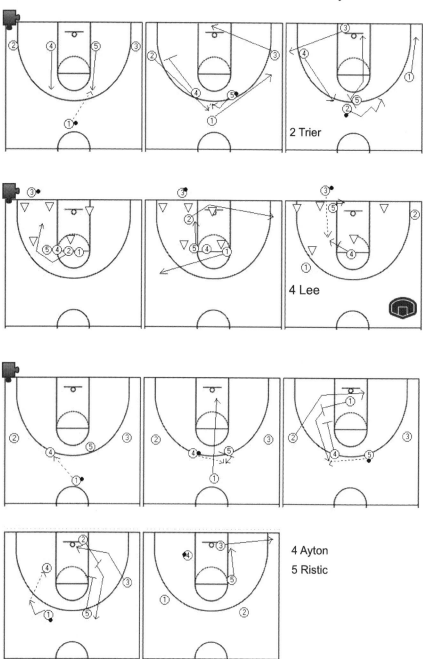

2 Trier

4 Lee

4 Ayton
5 Ristic

Arizona Wildcats

NCAA Basketball offense   Plays 2017-2018

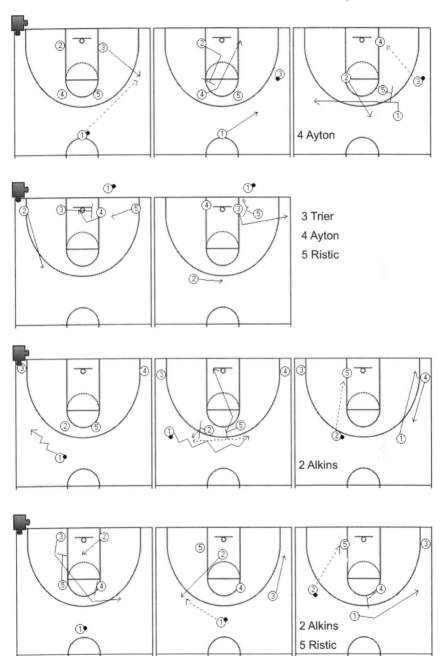

Arizona Wildcats

NCAA Basketball offense   Plays 2017-2018

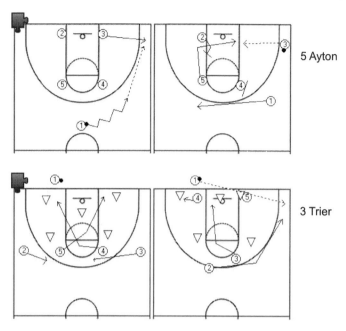

5 Ayton

3 Trier

Arizona Wildcats   20

NCAA Basketball offense　　　　　　　Plays 2017-2018

PAC - 12

ARIZONA STATE SUN DEVILS

Roster

#	Name	Position	Status
0	Tra Holder	Point Guard	Starter Star
1	Remy Martin	Point Guard	
2	Rob Edwards		
3	Mickey Mitchell	Power Forward	
10	Vitaliy Shibel	Power Forward	Starter
11	Shannon Evans II	Shooting Guard	Starter
14	Kimani Lawrence	Power Forward	
15	Carlton Bragg		
21	Jack Roggin		
22	Austin Witherill		
23	Romello White	Center	Starter
24	Jordan Salzman		
25	Grant Fogerty		
31	Zylan Cheatham		
34	Trevor Thompson		
35	De´quon Lake	Center	
44	Kodi Justice	Small Forward	Starter

Head coach　　　　　Bobby Hurley
Asociate H. coach　　Rashon Burno
Assistant coach　　　Levi Watkins
Assistant coach　　　Anthony Coleman

21

NCAA Basketball offense   Plays 2017-2018

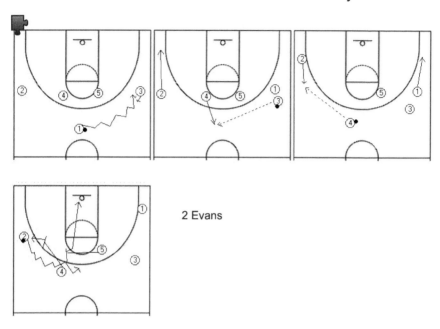

2 Evans

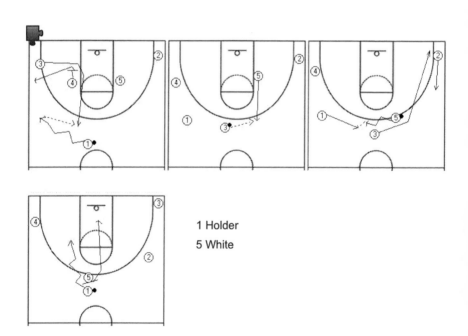

1 Holder
5 White

Arizona State Sun Devils

NCAA Basketball offense — Plays 2017-2018

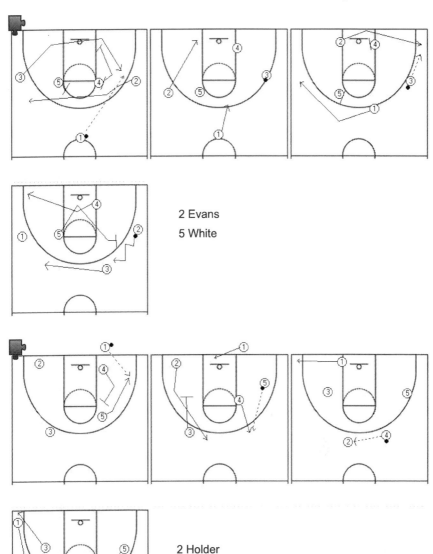

2 Evans
5 White

2 Holder
5 White
4 Justice

Arizona State Sun Devils 23

NCAA Basketball offense — Plays 2017-2018

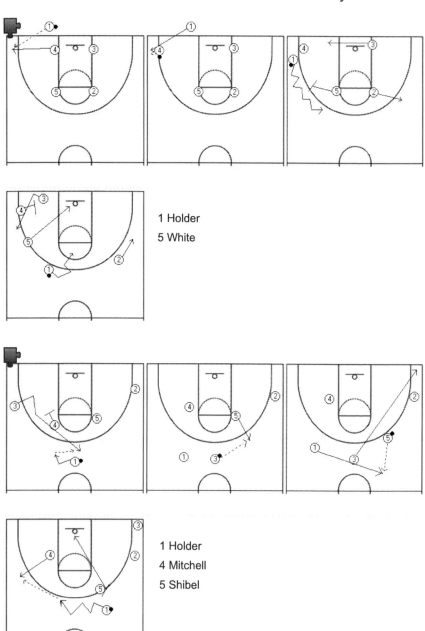

1 Holder
5 White

1 Holder
4 Mitchell
5 Shibel

Arizona State Sun Devils

NCAA Basketball offense — Plays 2017-2018

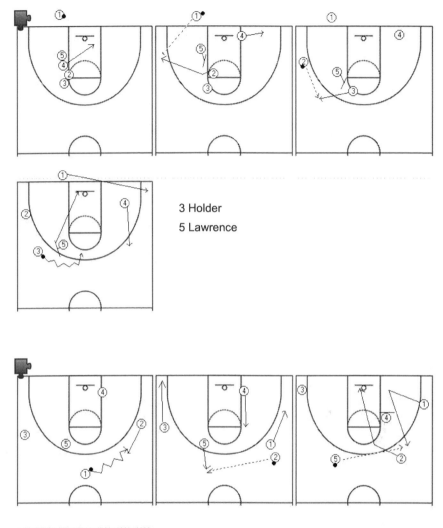

3 Holder
5 Lawrence

2 Holder
3 Evans II

Arizona State Sun Devils

NCAA Basketball offense — Plays 2017-2018

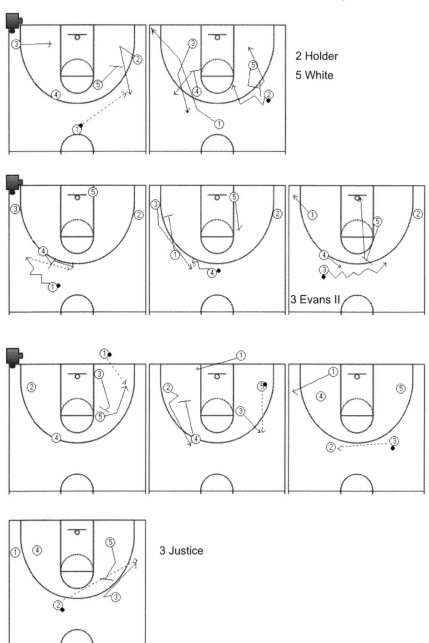

2 Holder
5 White

3 Evans II

3 Justice

Arizona State Sun Devils

NCAA Basketball offense   Plays 2017-2018

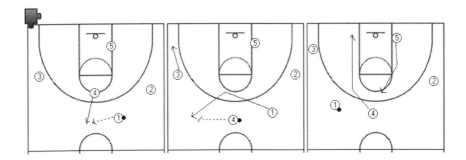

1 Holder
5 White
4 Justice

Arizona State Sun Devils   27

NCAA Basketball offense — Plays 2017-2018

BIG 12

BAYLOR BEARS

Roster

#	Name	Position	
0	Jo Lual-Acuil Jr	Power Forward	Starter Star
3	Jake Lindsey	Point Guard	
4	Mario Kegler	Small Forward	
10	Tyson Jolly	Small Forward	
11	Mark Vital	Small Forward	
12	Leonard Allen	Power Forward	
20	Manu Lecomte	Point Guard	Starter
21	Nuni Omot	Small Forward	Starter
22	King McClure	Shooting Guard	Starter
25	Tristan Clark	Center	Starter
30	Jonathan Davis		
31	Terry Maston	Power Forward	
45	Freddie Gillespie		
50	Obim Okeke		

Head coach — Scott Drew
Asociate H. coach — Jerome Tang
Assistant coach — Alvin Brooks III
Assistant coach — John Jakus

NCAA Basketball offense — Plays 2017-2018

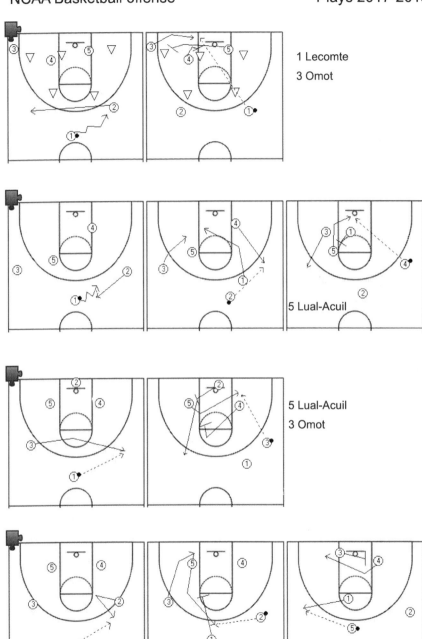

1 Lecomte
3 Omot

5 Lual-Acuil

5 Lual-Acuil
3 Omot

4 Clark

Baylor Bears

NCAA Basketball offense   Plays 2017-2018

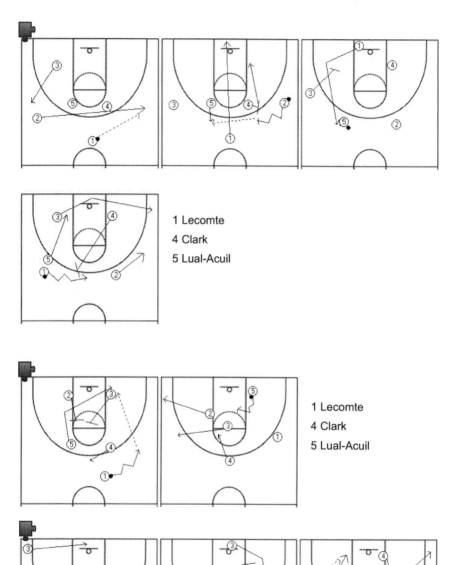

1 Lecomte
4 Clark
5 Lual-Acuil

1 Lecomte
4 Clark
5 Lual-Acuil

5 Lual-Acuil

Baylor Bears   30

NCAA Basketball offense   Plays 2017-2018

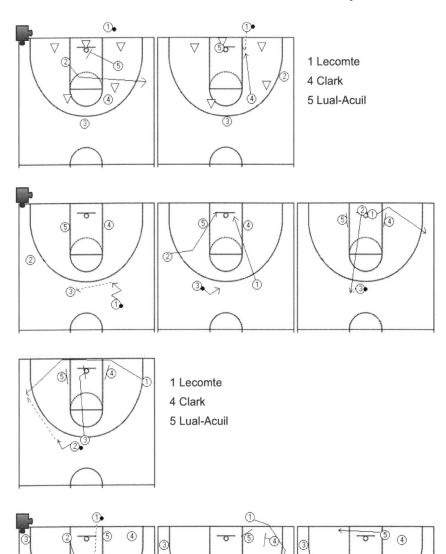

1 Lecomte
4 Clark
5 Lual-Acuil

1 Lecomte
4 Clark
5 Lual-Acuil

1 Lecomte

Baylor Bears   31

NCAA Basketball offense   Plays 2017-2018

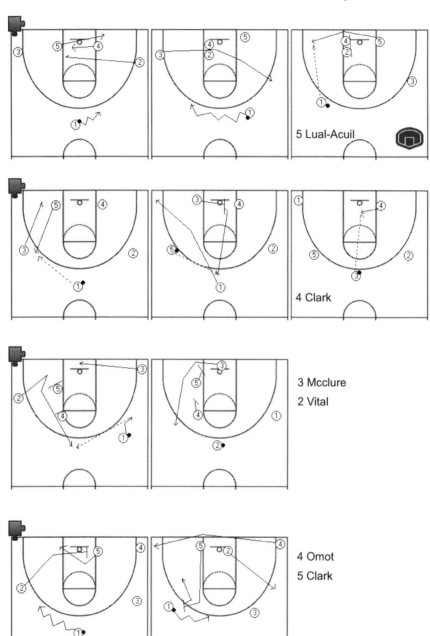

5 Lual-Acuil

4 Clark

3 Mcclure
2 Vital

4 Omot
5 Clark

Baylor Bears

NCAA Basketball offense

Plays 2017-2018

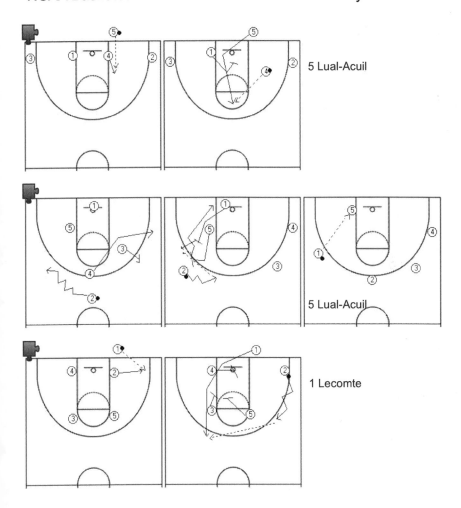

5 Lual-Acuil

5 Lual-Acuil

1 Lecomte

Baylor Bears 33

NCAA Basketball offense — Plays 2017-2018

American Athletic Conference

CINCINNATI BEARCATS

Roster

#	Name	Position	Status
1	Jacob Evans III	Shooting Guard	Starter
2	Keith Williams		
3	Justin Jenifer	Point Guard	Starter
5	Trevor Moore	Shooting Guard	
11	Gary Clark	Power Forward	Starter
13	Tre Scott		
14	Jackson Bart		
15	Cane Broome	Point Guard	
20	Mamoudou Diarra		
22	Eliel Nsoseme	Center	
24	Kyle Washington	Power Forward	Starter
31	Sam Martin		
32	John Koz		
33	Nysier Brooks	Center	
34	Jarrod Cumberland	Small Forward	Starter

Head coach	Mick Cronin
Asociate H. coach	Larry Davis
Assistant coach	Darren Savino
Assistant coach	Antwon Jackson

NCAA Basketball offense — Plays 2017-2018

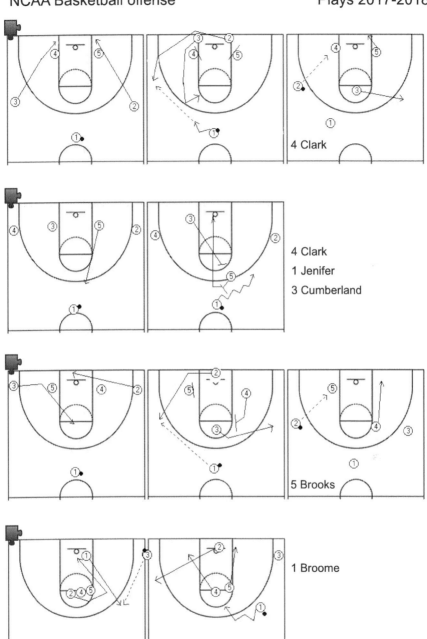

4 Clark

4 Clark
1 Jenifer
3 Cumberland

5 Brooks

1 Broome

Cincinnati Bearcats

NCAA Basketball offense — Plays 2017-2018

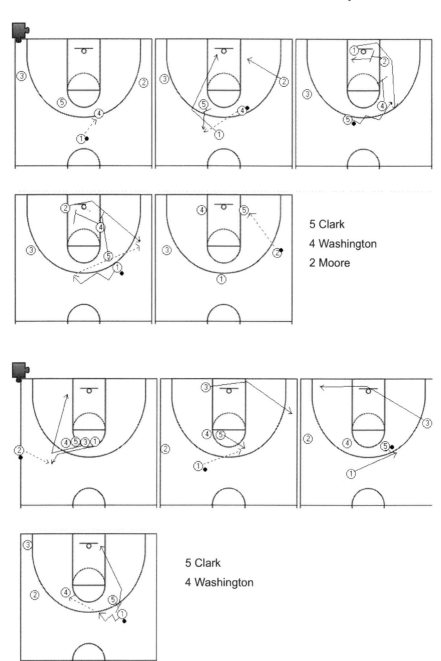

5 Clark
4 Washington
2 Moore

5 Clark
4 Washington

Cincinnati Bearcats

NCAA Basketball offense   Plays 2017-2018

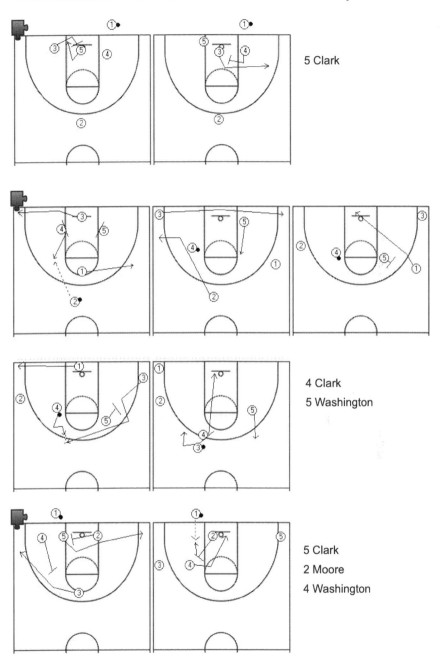

5 Clark

4 Clark
5 Washington

5 Clark
2 Moore
4 Washington

Cincinnati Bearcats

NCAA Basketball offense   Plays 2017-2018

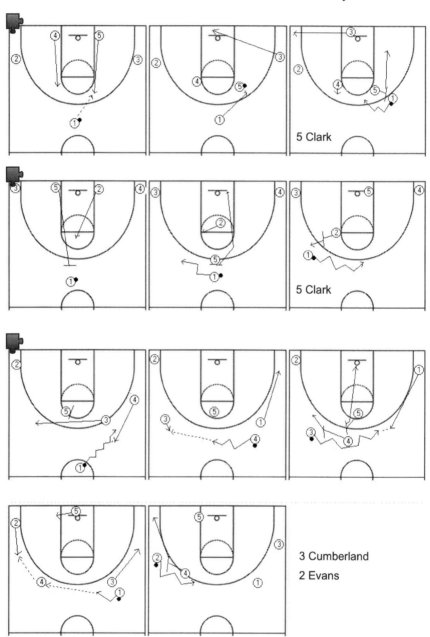

5 Clark

5 Clark

3 Cumberland
2 Evans

Cincinnati Bearcats

NCAA Basketball offense   Plays 2017-2018

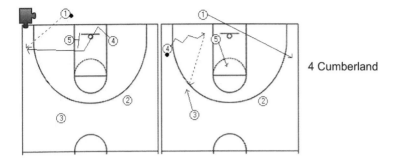

4 Cumberland

Cincinnati Bearcats   39

NCAA Basketball offense Plays 2017-2018

Atlantic Coast Conference ACC

DUKE BLUE DEVILS

Roster

#	Name	Position	Role
1	Trevon Duvall	Point Guard	Starter Star
2	Gary Trent Jr.	Shooting Guard	Starter Star
3	Grayson Allen	Shooting Guard	Starter Scorer
5	Jordan Tucker		
12	Javin DeLaurier	Power Forward	
14	Jordan Goldwire	Point Guard	
15	Alex O'Connell	Small Forward	
20	Marques Bolden	Center	
30	Antonio Vrankovic	Center	
34	Wendell Carter Jr.	Power Forward	Starter Star
35	Marvin Bagley III	Power Forward	Starter Star
41	Jack White	Small Forward	
50	Justin Robinson		
51	Mike Buckmire		
53	Brennan Besser		

Head coach	Mike Krzyzewski
Asociate H. coach	Jeff Capel
Assistant coach	Nate James
Assistant coach	Jon Scheyer
Special assistant	Nolan Smith

NCAA Basketball offense — Plays 2017-2018

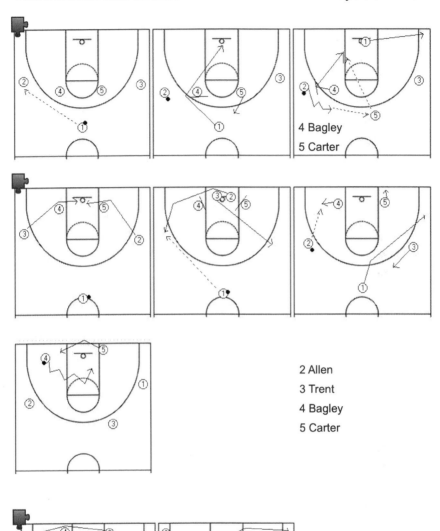

4 Bagley
5 Carter

2 Allen
3 Trent
4 Bagley
5 Carter

5 Bagley
3 Allen

Duke Blue Devils

NCAA Basketball offense

Plays 2017-2018

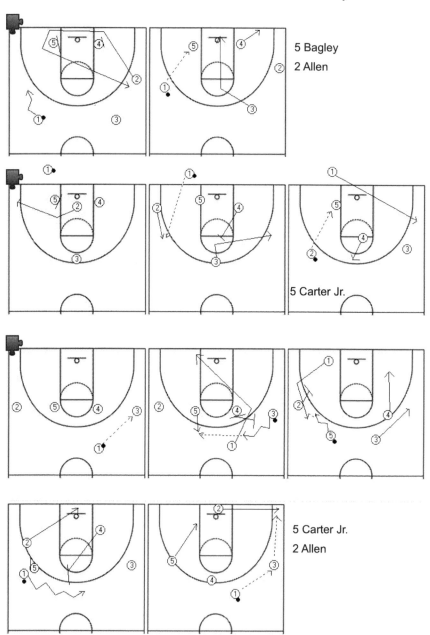

5 Bagley
2 Allen

5 Carter Jr.

5 Carter Jr.
2 Allen

Duke Blue Devils

NCAA Basketball offense — Plays 2017-2018

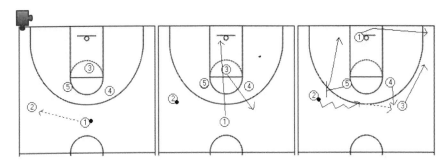

3 Bagley
4 Carter Jr.
5 Bolden

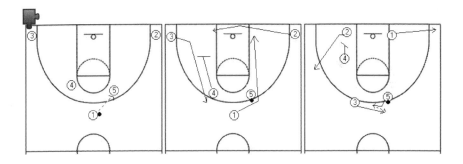

4 Bagley
5 Carter Jr.
3 Allen

Duke Blue Devils

NCAA Basketball offense — Plays 2017-2018

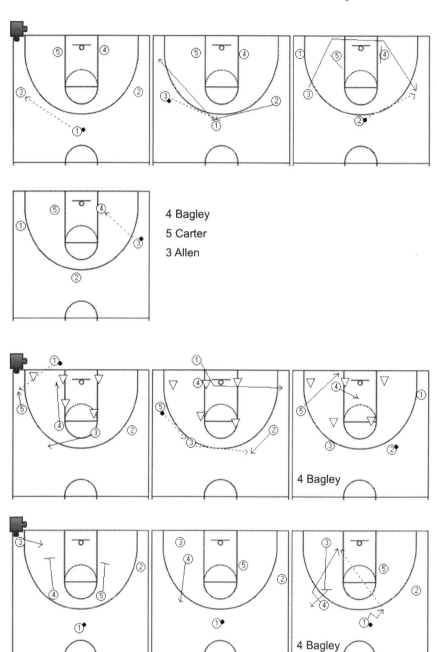

4 Bagley
5 Carter
3 Allen

4 Bagley

4 Bagley

Duke Blue Devils

NCAA Basketball offense   Plays 2017-2018

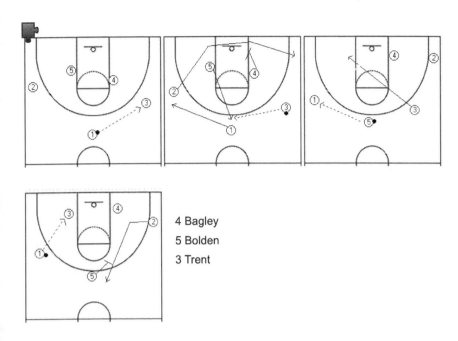

4 Bagley
5 Bolden
3 Trent

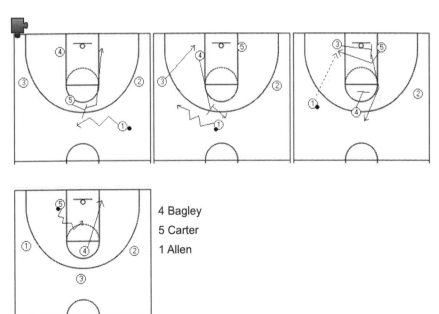

4 Bagley
5 Carter
1 Allen

Duke Blue Devils   45

NCAA Basketball offense   Plays 2017-2018

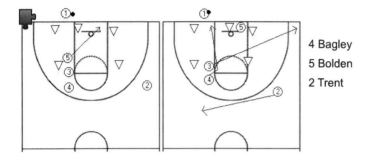

4 Bagley
5 Bolden
2 Trent

Duke Blue Devils

NCAA Basketball offense — Plays 2017-2018

SEC Conference

FLORIDA GATORS

Roster

#	Name	Position	Role
0	Mike Okauru		
1	Chase Johnson		
2	Isaiah Stokes		
3	Jalen Hudson	Shooting Guard	Starter Scorer
4	Egor Koulechov	Power Forward	Starter Scorer
5	KeVaughn Allen	Small Forward	Starter
11	Chris Chiozza	Point Guard	Starter
12	Gorjok Gak	Power Forward	
13	Kevarrius Hayes	Power Forward	
14	Mak Krause		
15	John Egbunu	Center	
21	Dontay Bassett		
22	Andrew Fava		
24	Deaundrae Ballard	Power Forward	
25	Keith Stone	Power Forward	Starter

Head coach   Mike White
Assistant coach   Dusty May
Assistant coach   Jordan Mincy
Assistant coach   Darris Nichols

NCAA Basketball offense   Plays 2017-2018

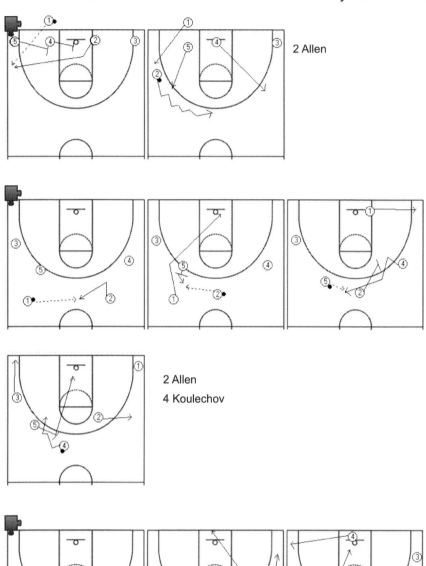

2 Allen

2 Allen
4 Koulechov

2 Hudson

Florida Gators   48

NCAA Basketball offense — Plays 2017-2018

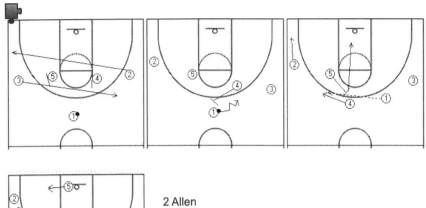

2 Allen
4 Koulechov

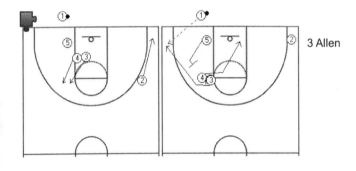

3 Allen

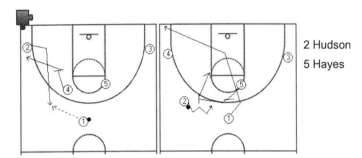

2 Hudson
5 Hayes

Florida Gators

NCAA Basketball offense — Plays 2017-2018

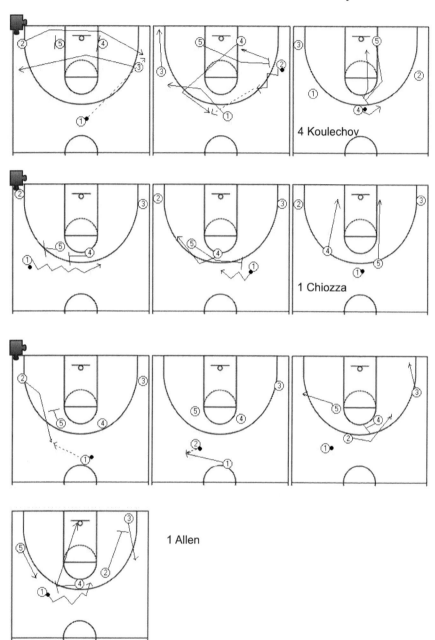

4 Koulechov

1 Chiozza

1 Allen

Florida Gators

NCAA Basketball offense   Plays 2017-2018

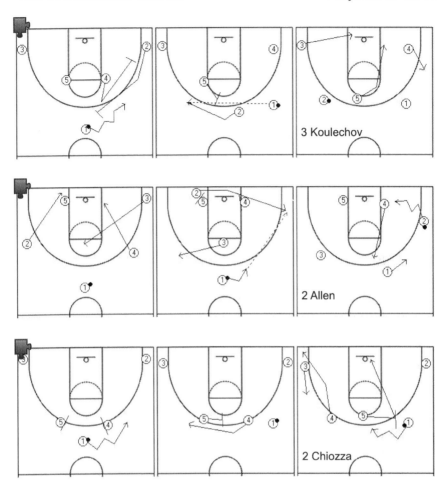

Florida Gators

NCAA Basketball offense — Plays 2017-2018

ACC Conference

FLORIDA STATE SEMINOLES

Roster

#	Name	Position	
0	Phil Cofer	Small Forward	Starter
1	Raiquan Gray		
2	C.J. Walker	Point Guard	Starter
3	Trent Forrest	Point Guard	
5	P.J. Savoy		
11	Brian Angola	Shooting Guard	Starter
12	Ike Obiagu	Center	Starter
13	Anthony Polite		
14	Terance Mann	Small Forward	Starter
15	Justin Lindner		
20	Travis Light		
21	Christ Koumadje	Center	
23	M.J. Walker	Shooting Guard	
25	Mfiondu Kabengele		
31	Wyatt Wilkes		
33	Will Miles		
35	Harrison Prieto		
40	Brandon Allen		

Head coach	Leonard Hamilton
A. Head coach	Stan Jones
Assistant coach	Charlton Young
Assistant coach	Dennis Gates

NCAA Basketball offense — Plays 2017-2018

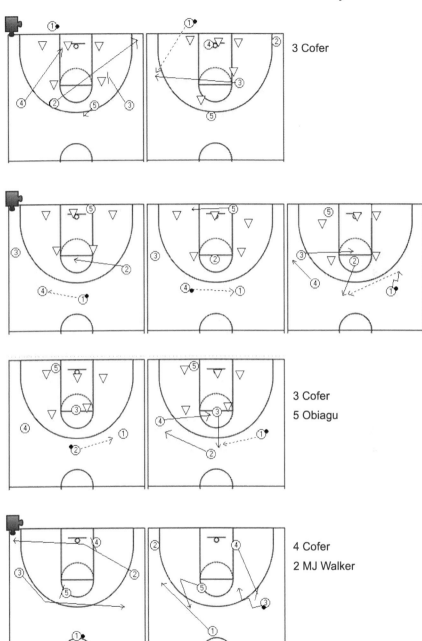

3 Cofer

3 Cofer
5 Obiagu

4 Cofer
2 MJ Walker

Florida State Seminoles

NCAA Basketball offense — Plays 2017-2018

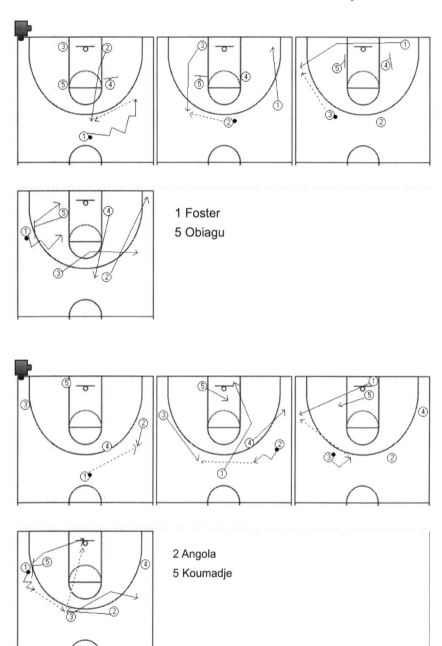

1 Foster
5 Obiagu

2 Angola
5 Koumadje

Florida State Seminoles

NCAA Basketball offense — Plays 2017-2018

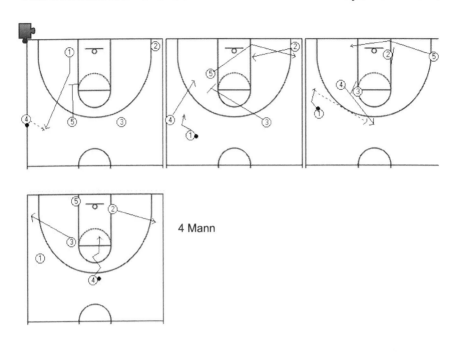

4 Mann

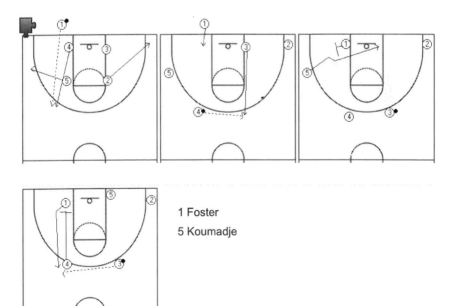

1 Foster
5 Koumadje

Florida State Seminoles

NCAA Basketball offense   Plays 2017-2018

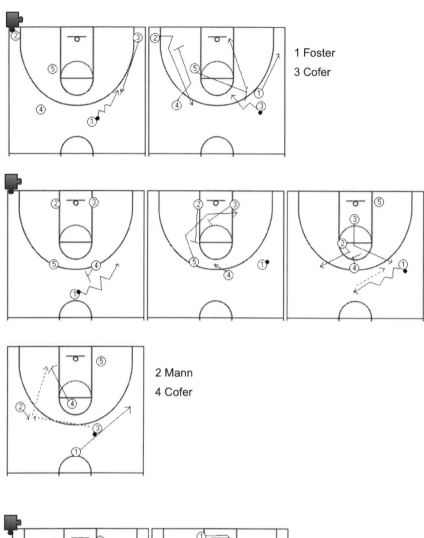

1 Foster
3 Cofer

2 Mann
4 Cofer

2 Walker

Florida State Seminoles

NCAA Basketball offense   Plays 2017-2018

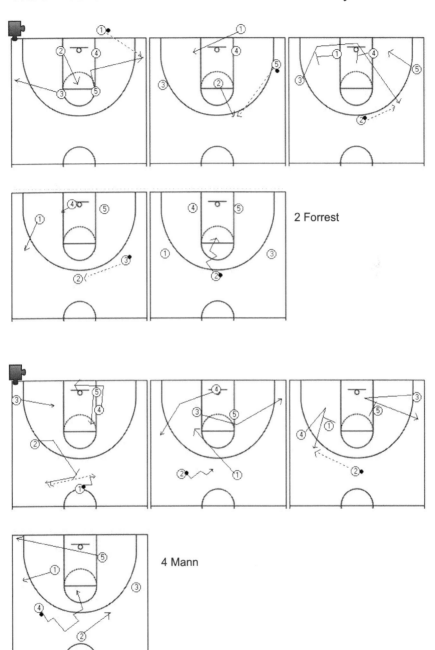

2 Forrest

4 Mann

Florida State Seminoles

NCAA Basketball offense — Plays 2017-2018

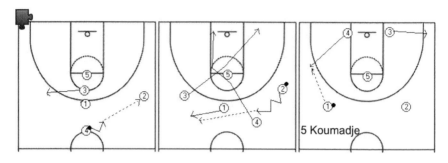

5 Koumadje

Florida State Seminoles 58

NCAA Basketball offense   Plays 2017-2018

West Coast Conference

GONZAGA BULLDOGS

Roster

#	Name	Position	Role
0	Silas Melson	Shooting Guard	Starter
2	Jack Beach		
3	Johnathan Williams	Power Forward	Starter
5	Alex Martin		
10	Jesse Wade		
11	Joel Ayayi		
13	Josh Perkins	Point Guard	Starter Star
14	Jacob Larsen	Center	
15	Brandon Clarke		
20	Brian Pete		
21	Rui Hachimura	Power Forward	
22	Jeremy Jones		
23	Zach Norvell Jr.	Small Forward	Starter
24	Corey Kispert	Small Forward	
33	Killian Tillie	Power Forward	Starter

Head coach	Mark Few
Assistant coach	Tommy Lloyd
Assistant coach	Donny Daniels
Assistant coach	Brian Michaelson

NCAA Basketball offense   Plays 2017-2018

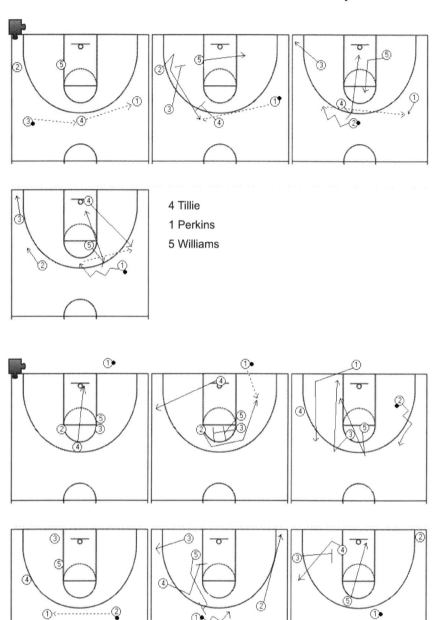

4 Tillie
1 Perkins
5 Williams

Gonzaga Bulldogs

NCAA Basketball offense   Plays 2017-2018

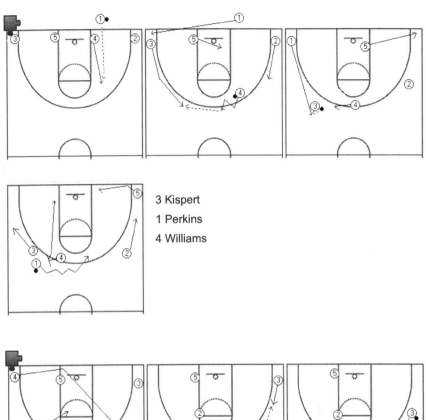

3 Kispert
1 Perkins
4 Williams

3 Kispert
1 Perkins
4 Hachimura

Gonzaga Bulldogs

NCAA Basketball offense   Plays 2017-2018

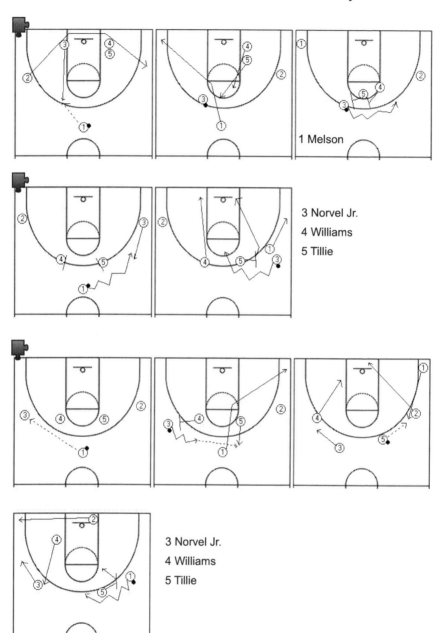

1 Melson

3 Norvel Jr.
4 Williams
5 Tillie

3 Norvel Jr.
4 Williams
5 Tillie

Gonzaga Bulldogs

NCAA Basketball offense   Plays 2017-2018

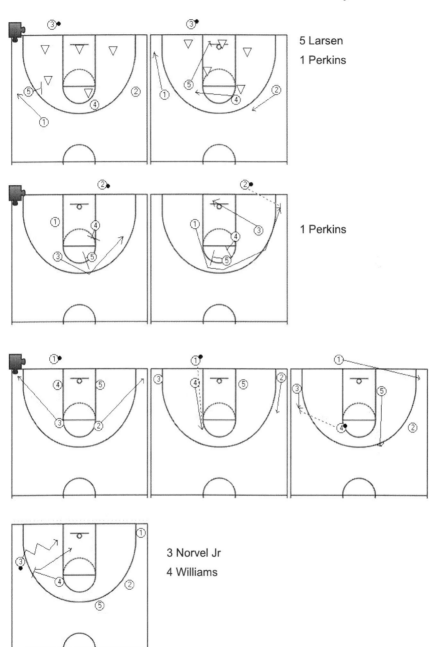

5 Larsen
1 Perkins

1 Perkins

3 Norvel Jr
4 Williams

Gonzaga Bulldogs

NCAA Basketball offense — Plays 2017-2018

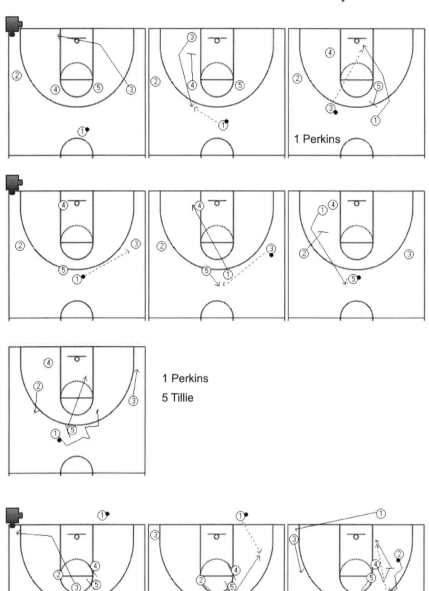

1 Perkins

1 Perkins
5 Tillie

4 Williams

Gonzaga Bulldogs

NCAA Basketball offense — Plays 2017-2018

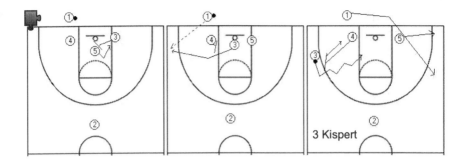

3 Kispert

Gonzaga Bulldogs

NCAA Basketball offense — Plays 2017-2018

Big 12

KANSAS JAYHAWKS

Roster

#	Name	Position	
0	Marcus Garrett	Small Forward	
1	Dedric Lawson	Shooting Guard	
2	Lagerald Vick	Small Forward	Starter Star
3	Sam Cunliffe	Shooting Guard	
4	Devonte Graham	Point Guard	Starter Scorer
5	Charlie Moore		
10	Sviatoslav Mykhailiuk	Small Forward	Starter Shooter
12	Chris Teahan		
13	K. J. Lawson	Small Forward	
14	Malik Newman	Shooting Guard	Starter
21	Clay Young	Power Forward	
23	Billy Preston	Center	
35	Udoka Azubuike	Center	Starter powerful
44	Mitch Lightfoot	Power Forward	

Head coach — Bill Self
Assistant coach — Kurtis Townsend
Assistant coach — Norm Roberts
Assistant coach — Jerrance Howard

NCAA Basketball offense — Plays 2017-2018

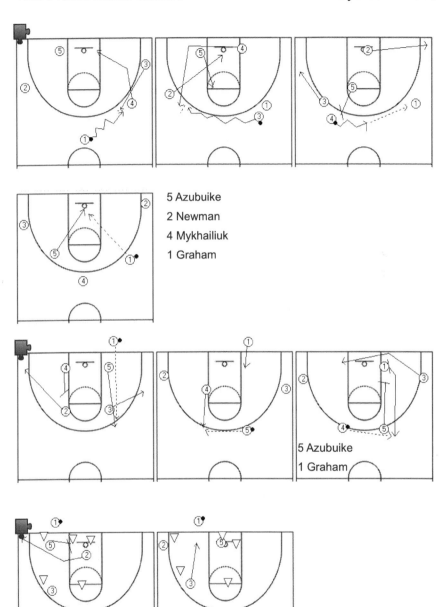

5 Azubuike
2 Newman
4 Mykhailiuk
1 Graham

5 Azubuike
1 Graham

5 Azubuike
3 Vick

Kansas Jayhawks

NCAA Basketball offense — Plays 2017-2018

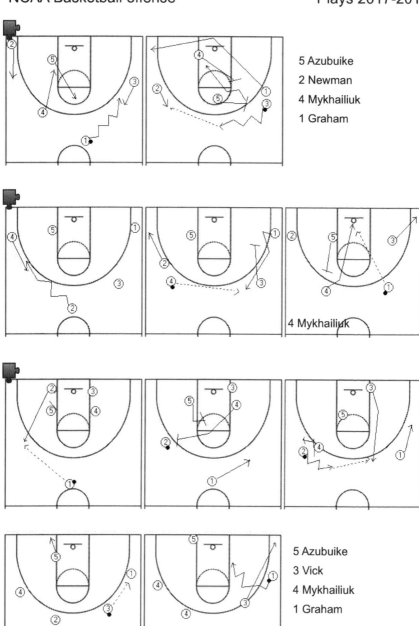

5 Azubuike
2 Newman
4 Mykhailiuk
1 Graham

4 Mykhailiuk

5 Azubuike
3 Vick
4 Mykhailiuk
1 Graham

Kansas Jayhawks

NCAA Basketball offense — Plays 2017-2018

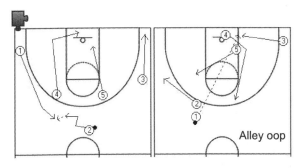

5 Azubuike
2 Newman
4 Mykhailiuk
1 Graham

Alley oop

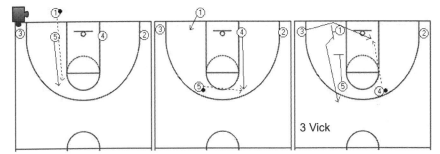

3 Vick

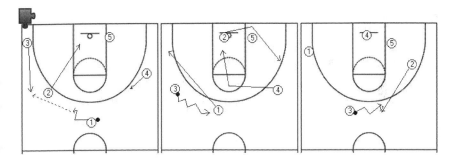

2 Newman
4 Mykhailiuk
1 Graham

Kansas Jayhawks

NCAA Basketball offense — Plays 2017-2018

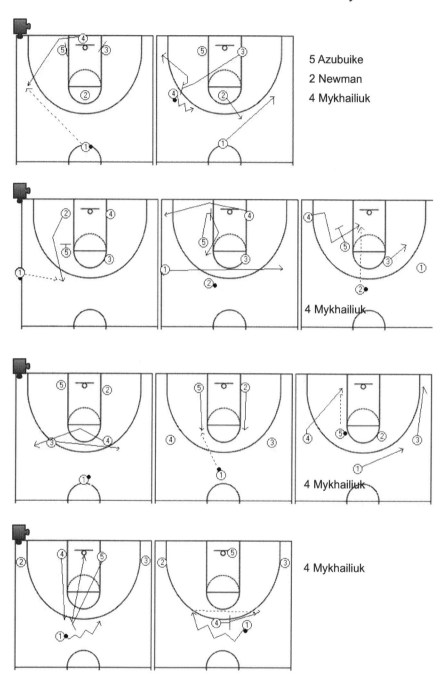

5 Azubuike
2 Newman
4 Mykhailiuk

4 Mykhailiuk

4 Mykhailiuk

4 Mykhailiuk

Kansas Jayhawks

NCAA Basketball offense   Plays 2017-2018

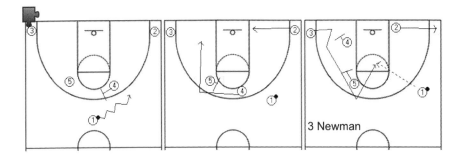

3 Newman

Kansas Jayhawks

NCAA Basketball offense Plays 2017-2018

Southeastern Conference SEC

KENTUCKY WILDCATS

Roster

#	Name	Position	Role
0	Quade Green	Point Guard	Starter
1	Sacha Killeya-Jones	Shooting Guard	
2	Jarred Vanderbilt		
3	Hamidou Diallo	Small Forward	Starter
4	Nick Richards	Power Forward	
5	Kevin Knox	Small Forward	Starter Star
10	Jonny David		
12	Brad Calipari		
13	Jemarl Baker		
14	Tai Wynyard	Shooting Guard	
22	Shai Gilgeous-Alexander	Shooting Guard	
25	PJ Washington	Power Forward	Starter
30	Dillon Pulliam		
32	Wenyen Gabriel	Power Forward	Starter

Head coach	John Calipari
Assistant coach	Tony Barbee
Assistant coach	Joel Justus
Associate H. coach	Kenny Payne
Special assistant h. coach	John Robic

NCAA Basketball offense — Plays 2017-2018

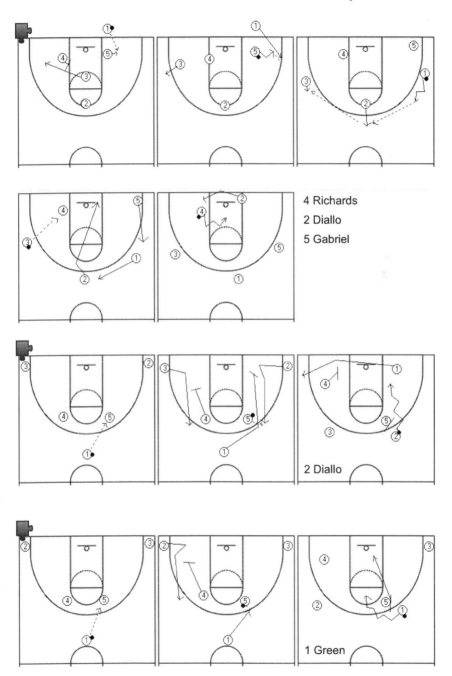

4 Richards
2 Diallo
5 Gabriel

2 Diallo

1 Green

Kentucky Wildcats

NCAA Basketball offense — Plays 2017-2018

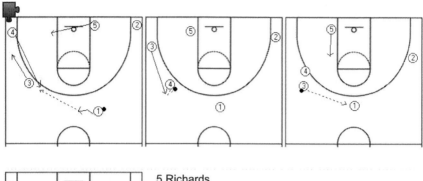

5 Richards
2 Diallo
4 Gabriel
3 Knox

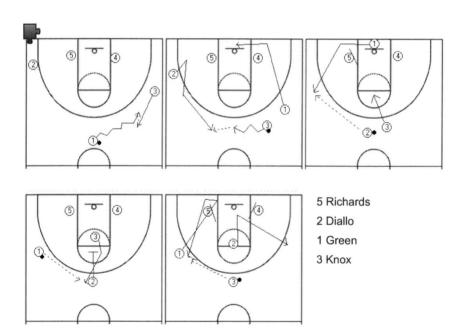

5 Richards
2 Diallo
1 Green
3 Knox

Kentucky Wildcats

NCAA Basketball offense   Plays 2017-2018

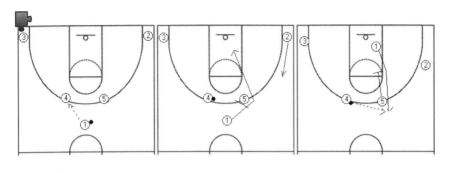

5 Richards
2 Diallo
1 Green
3 Knox

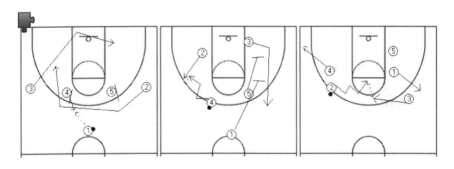

5 Richards
2 Diallo
1 Green
3 Knox

Kentucky Wildcats

NCAA Basketball offense — Plays 2017-2018

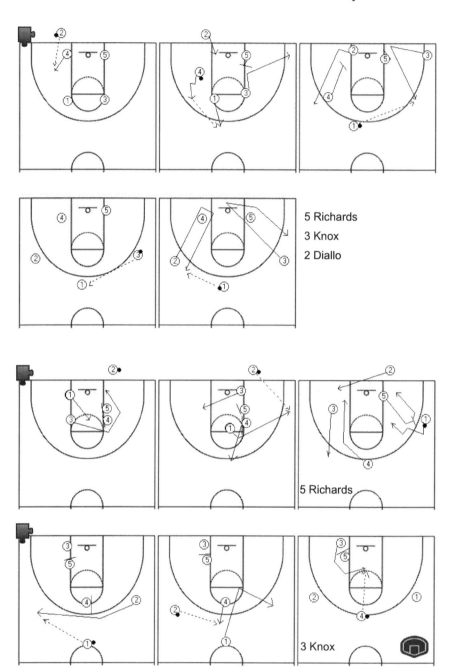

5 Richards
3 Knox
2 Diallo

5 Richards

3 Knox

Kentucky Wildcats

NCAA Basketball offense — Plays 2017-2018

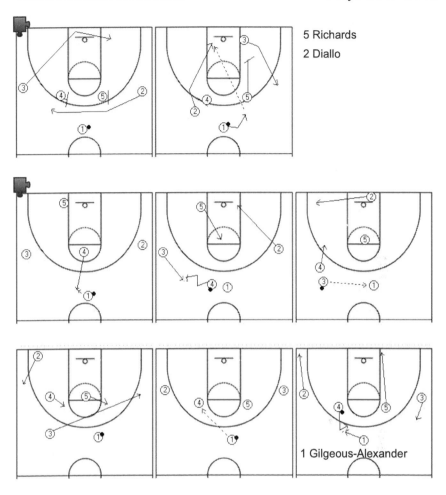

5 Richards
2 Diallo

1 Gilgeous-Alexander

Kentucky Wildcats

NCAA Basketball offense Plays 2017-2018

Atlantic Coast Conference

MIAMI HURRICANES

Roster

0	Ja´Quan Newton	Point Guard	Starter
1	Dejan Vasiljevic	Shooting Guard	
2	Chris Lykes	Point Guard	
3	Anthony Lawrence II	Power Forward	Starter
4	Lonnie Walker IV	Small Forward	Starter
5	Mike Robinson		
10	Miles Wilson		
11	Bruce Brown Jr.	Small Forward	Starter Star
14	Rodney Miller Jr.	Center	
15	Ebuka Izundu	Center	
20	Dewan Huell	Center	Starter
21	Sam Waardenburg	Power Forward	
22	Deng Gak		
35	Chris Stowell		

Head coach	Jim Larrañaga
A. Head coach	Chris Caputo
Assistant coach	Jamal Brunt
Assistant coach	Adam Fisher

NCAA Basketball offense — Plays 2017-2018

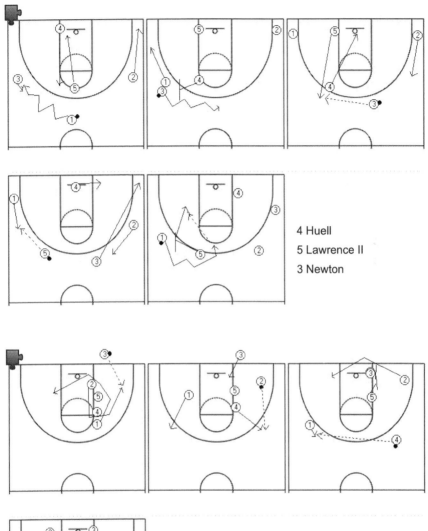

4 Huell
5 Lawrence II
3 Newton

2 Vasiljevic
5 Huell
3 Newton

Miami Hurricanes

NCAA Basketball offense — Plays 2017-2018

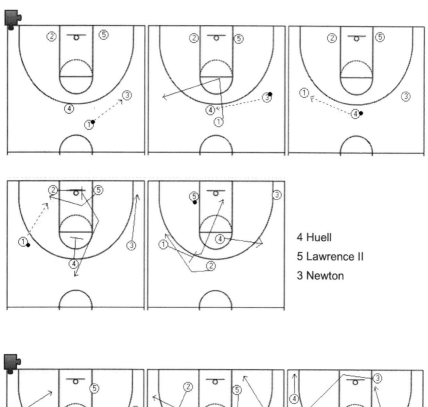

4 Huell
5 Lawrence II
3 Newton

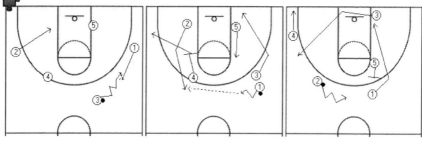

2 Vasiljevic
5 Huell
3 Newton

Miami Hurricanes

NCAA Basketball offense   Plays 2017-2018

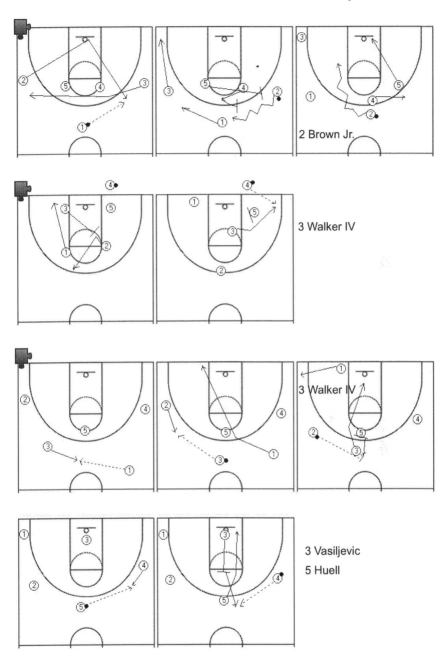

2 Brown Jr.

3 Walker IV

3 Walker IV

3 Vasiljevic
5 Huell

Miami Hurricanes

NCAA Basketball offense — Plays 2017-2018

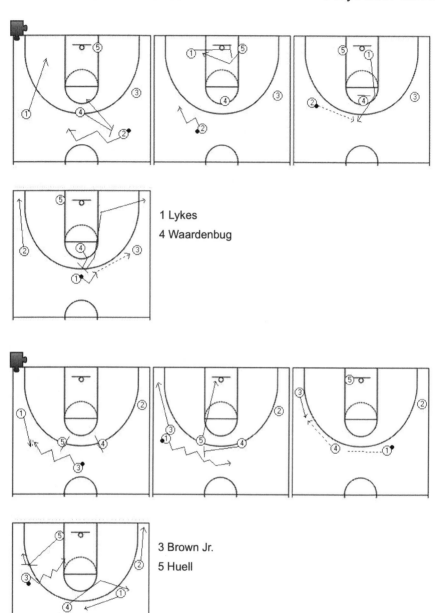

1 Lykes
4 Waardenbug

3 Brown Jr.
5 Huell

Miami Hurricanes

NCAA Basketball offense — Plays 2017-2018

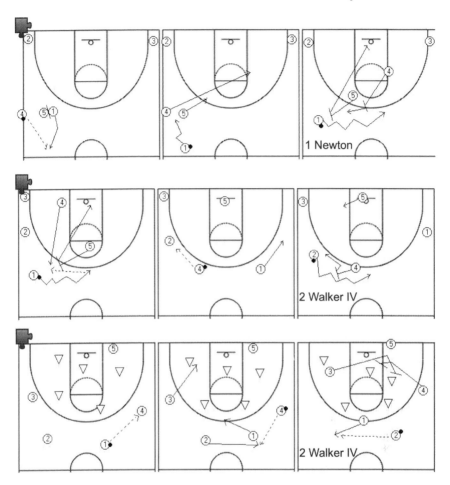

Miami Hurricanes

NCAA Basketball offense — Plays 2017-2018

Big Ten Conference

MICHIGAN STATE SPARTANS

Roster

#	Name	Position	Role
0	Kyle Ahrens	Point Guard	Starter Scorer
1	Joshua Langford	Shooting Guard	
2	Jaren Jackson Jr.	Power forward	Starter Star
5	Cassius Winston	Point Guard	Starter
10	Jack Hoiberg		
11	"Tum Tum" Nairn Jr.	Point Guard	
13	Ben Carter	Power Forward	
14	Brock Washington		
20	Matt McQuaid	Shooting Guard	
22	Miles Bridges	Small Forward	Starter Star
23	Xavier Tillman	Power Forward	
25	Kenny Goins	Power Forward	
34	Gavin Schilling	Center	
40	Braden Burke		
41	Conner George		
44	Nick Ward	Center	Starter

Head coach	Tom Izzo
Assistant coach	Dwayne Stephens
Assistant coach	Mike Garland
Assistant coach	Dane Fife

NCAA Basketball offense — Plays 2017-2018

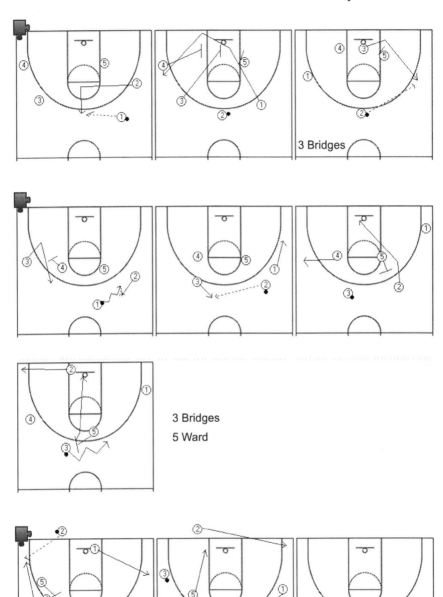

3 Bridges

3 Bridges
5 Ward

3 Bridges

Michigan State Spartans

NCAA Basketball offense — Plays 2017-2018

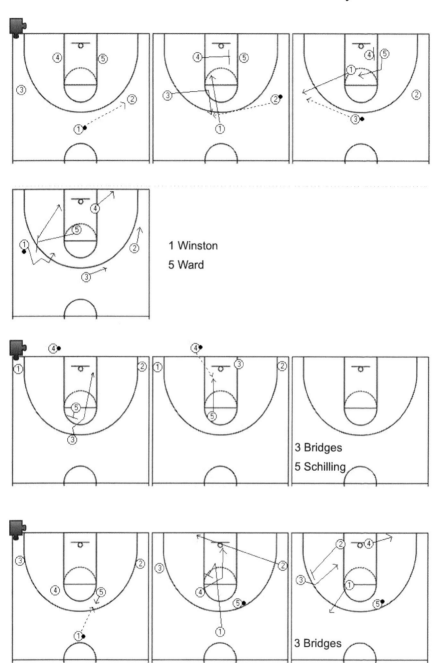

1 Winston
5 Ward

3 Bridges
5 Schilling

3 Bridges

Michigan State Spartans

NCAA Basketball offense — Plays 2017-2018

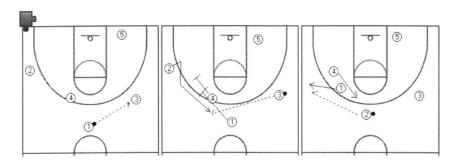

1 Winston
5 Schilling
4 Jaren Jackson Jr.

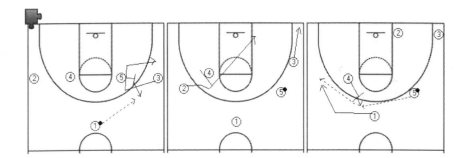

1 Winston
5 Ward
4 Jaren Jackson Jr.
3 Bridges

Michigan State Spartans

NCAA Basketball offense — Plays 2017-2018

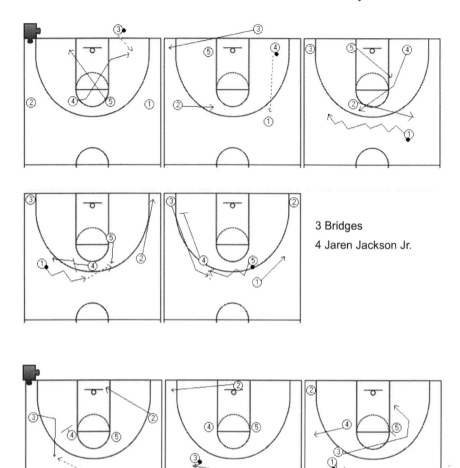

3 Bridges
4 Jaren Jackson Jr.

1 Winston
5 Ward
4 Jaren Jackson Jr.
3 Bridges

Michigan State Spartans

NCAA Basketball offense — Plays 2017-2018

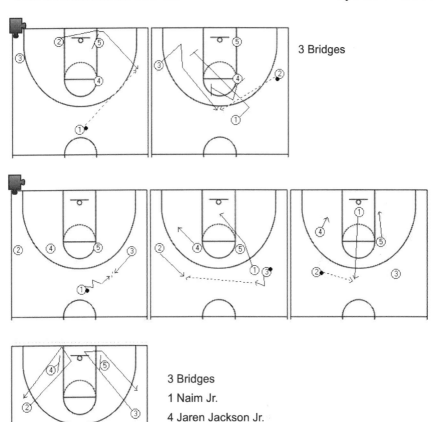

3 Bridges

3 Bridges
1 Naim Jr.
4 Jaren Jackson Jr.

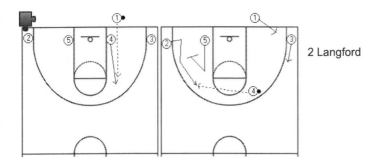

2 Langford

Michigan State Spartans

NCAA Basketball offense — Plays 2017-2018

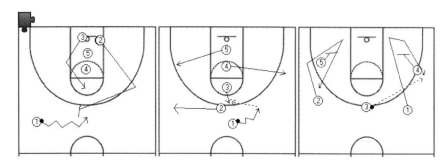

3 Bridges
1 Winston
4 Jaren Jackson Jr.

Michigan State Spartans

NCAA Basketball offense — Plays 2017-2018

Atlantic Coast Conference

MINNESOTA GOLDEN GOPHERS

Roster

#	Name	Position	
1	Dupree McBrayer	Shotting Guard	Starter
2	Nate Mason	Point Guard	Starter
3	Jordan Murphy	Power Forward	Starter Star
4	Jamir Harris		
5	Amir Coffey	Small Forward	Starter
10	Brady Rudrud		
11	Isaiah Washington		
12	Jarvis Johnson		
13	Hunt Conroy		
20	Davonte Fitzgerald	Power Forward	
21	Bakary Konaté	Center	
22	Reggie Lynch	Center	Starter
24	Eric Curry		
35	Matz Stockman	Center	
41	Gaston Diedhiou	Center	
42	Michael Hurt	Small Forward	

Head coach	Richard Pitino
Assistant coach	Ed Conroy
Assistant coach	Ben Johnson
Assistant coach	Kimani Young

NCAA Basketball offense   Plays 2017-2018

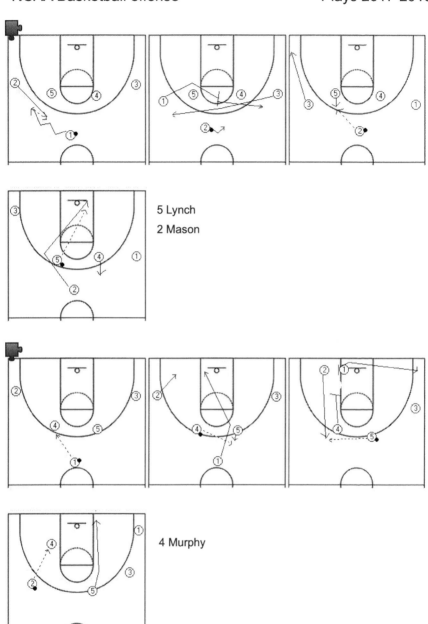

5 Lynch
2 Mason

4 Murphy

Minnesota Golden Gophers   92

NCAA Basketball offense — Plays 2017-2018

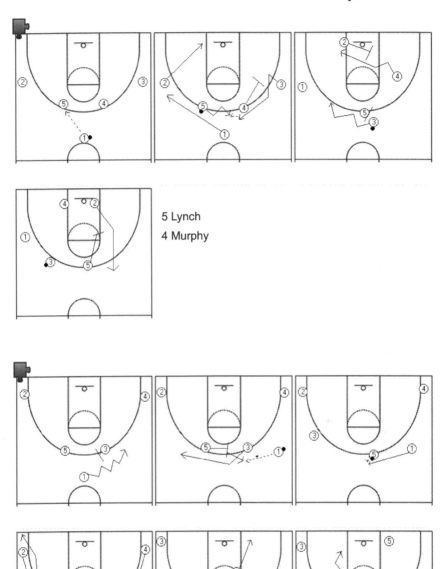

5 Lynch
4 Murphy

4 Murphy

Minnesota Golden Gophers

NCAA Basketball offense — Plays 2017-2018

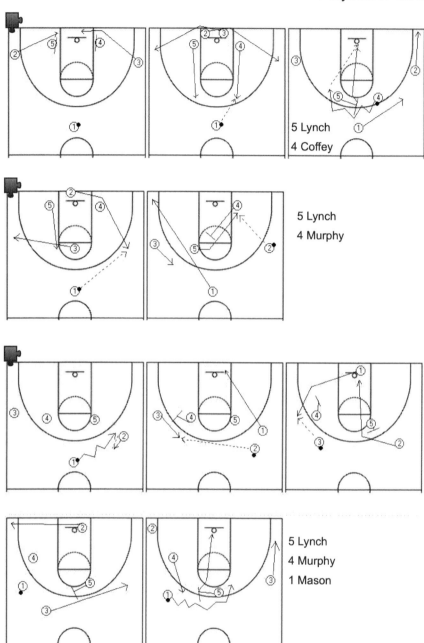

5 Lynch
4 Coffey

5 Lynch
4 Murphy

5 Lynch
4 Murphy
1 Mason

Minnesota Golden Gophers

NCAA Basketball offense — Plays 2017-2018

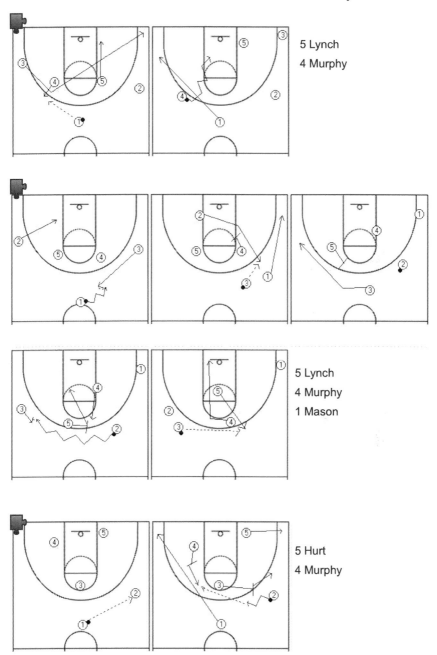

5 Lynch
4 Murphy

5 Lynch
4 Murphy
1 Mason

5 Hurt
4 Murphy

Minnesota Golden Gophers

NCAA Basketball offense — Plays 2017-2018

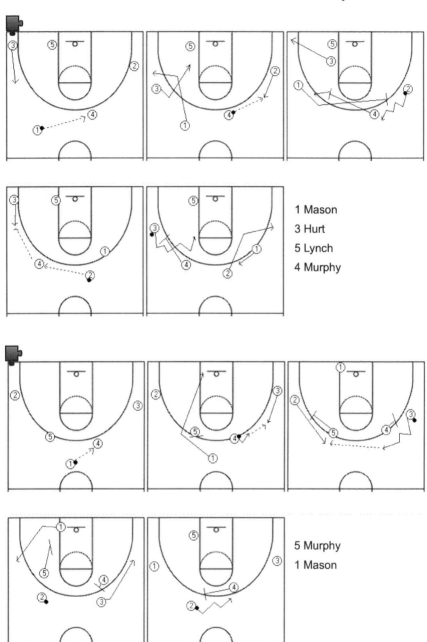

1 Mason
3 Hurt
5 Lynch
4 Murphy

5 Murphy
1 Mason

Minnesota Golden Gophers

NCAA Basketball offense — Plays 2017-2018

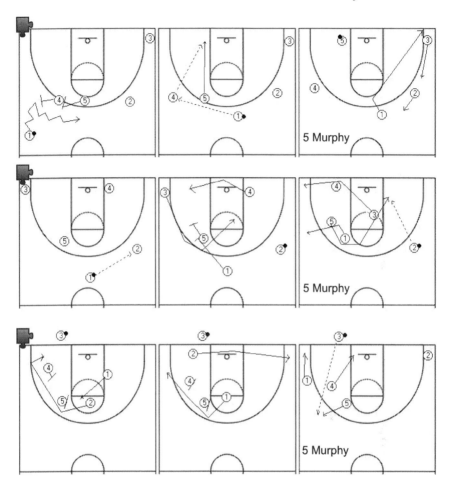

5 Murphy

Minnesota Golden Gophers

NCAA Basketball offense　　　　　　　Plays 2017-2018

Atlantic Coast Conference ACC

NORTH CAROLINA TAR HEELS

Roster

0	Seventh Woods	Point Guard	
1	Theo Pinson	Small Forward	Starter
2	Joel Berry II	Point Guard	Starter Star
3	Andrew Platek	Shooting Guard	
4	Brandon Robinson		
5	Jalek Felton	Point Guard	
11	Shea Rush		
13	Cameron Johnson	Small Forward	
15	Garrison Brooks	Power Forward	Starter
21	Sterling Manley		
22	Walker Miller		
24	Kenny Williams	Shooting Guard	Starter
25	Aaron Rohlman		
30	K.J. Smith		
32	Luke Maye	Center	Starter
42	Brandon Huffman	Center	

Head coach　　　　　　Roy Williams
Assistant coach　　　Steve Robinson
Assistant coach　　　　Hubert Davis
Assistant coach　　　Brad Frederick

NCAA Basketball offense — Plays 2017-2018

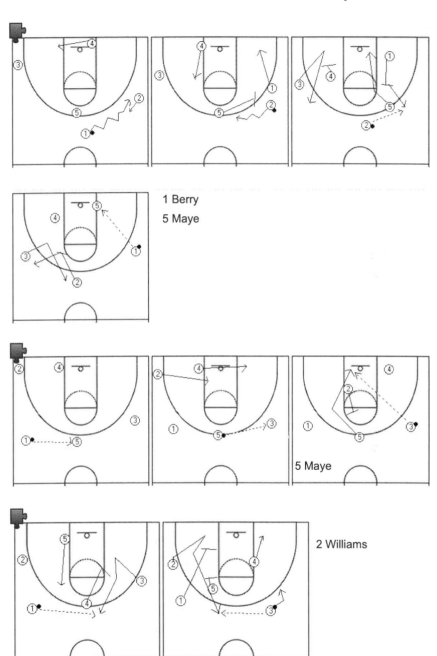

1 Berry
5 Maye

5 Maye

2 Williams

North Carolina Tar Heels

NCAA Basketball offense   Plays 2017-2018

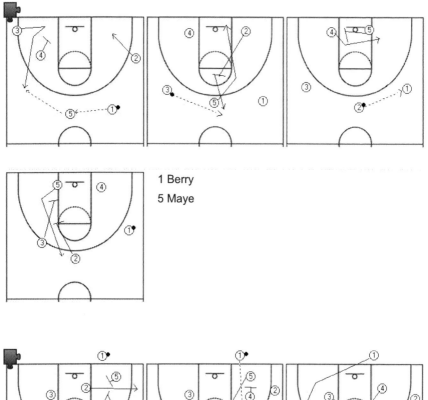

1 Berry
5 Maye

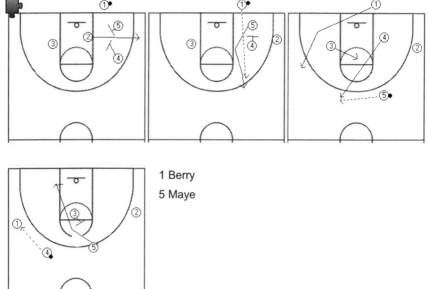

1 Berry
5 Maye

North Carolina Tar Heels   100

NCAA Basketball offense — Plays 2017-2018

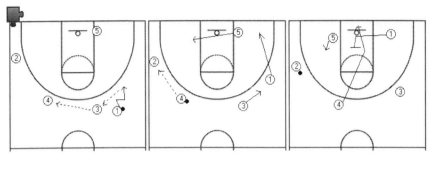

1 Berry
5 Maye
2 Williams

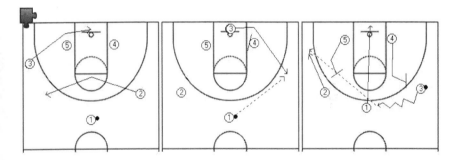

1 Berry
5 Maye
3 Johnson

North Carolina Tar Heels

NCAA Basketball offense — Plays 2017-2018

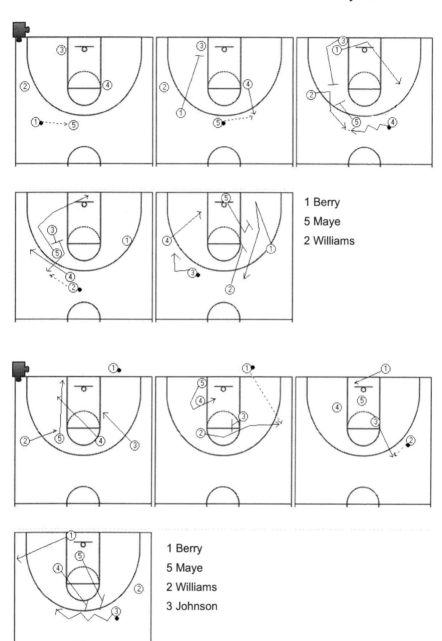

1 Berry
5 Maye
2 Williams

1 Berry
5 Maye
2 Williams
3 Johnson

North Carolina Tar Heels

NCAA Basketball offense   Plays 2017-2018

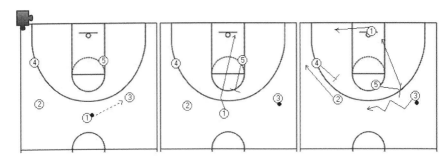

1 Berry
5 Brooks
2 Williams
3 Johnson

1 Berry
5 Maye
2 Williams
3 Johnson

North Carolina Tar Heels

NCAA Basketball offense — Plays 2017-2018

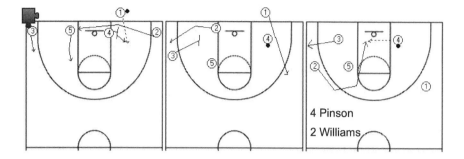

4 Pinson
2 Williams

North Carolina Tar Heels

NCAA Basketball offense　　　　　　Plays 2017-2018

Atlantic Coast Conference ACC

NOTRE DAME FIGHTING IRISH

Roster

0	Rex Pflueger	Small Forward	Starter
1	Austin Torres	Power Forward	
3	D.J. Harvey	Small Forward	
5	Matt Farrell	Point Guard	Starter Star
10	T. J. Gibbs Jr.	Shooting Guard	Starter
11	Juwan Durham		
12	Elijah Burns	Power Forward	
13	Nikola Djogo	Small Forward	
21	Matt Gregory		
23	Martinas Geben	Center	Starter
25	Liam Nelligan		
33	John Money	Center	
35	Bonzie Colson	Power Forward	Starter Star

Head coach　　　　　　Mike Brey
A. head coach　　　　　Rod Balanis
Assistant coach　　　　Ryan Ayers
Assistant coach　　　　Ryan Humphrey

NCAA Basketball offense — Plays 2017-2018

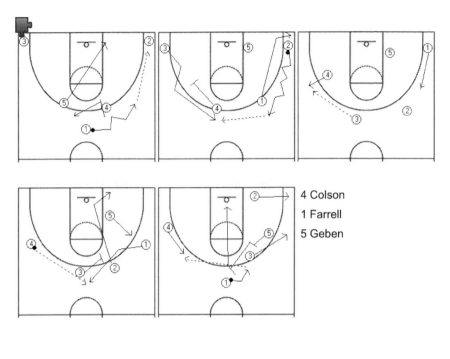

4 Colson
1 Farrell
5 Geben

4 Colson
1 Farrell
3 Pflueger
5 Geben

Notre Dame Fighting Irish

NCAA Basketball offense — Plays 2017-2018

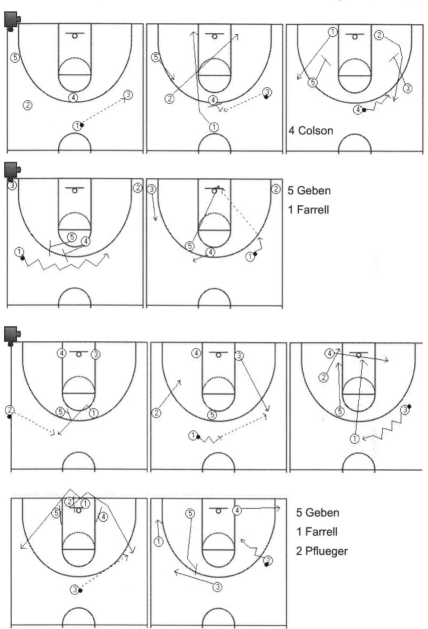

4 Colson

5 Geben
1 Farrell

5 Geben
1 Farrell
2 Pflueger

Notre Dame Fighting Irish

NCAA Basketball offense — Plays 2017-2018

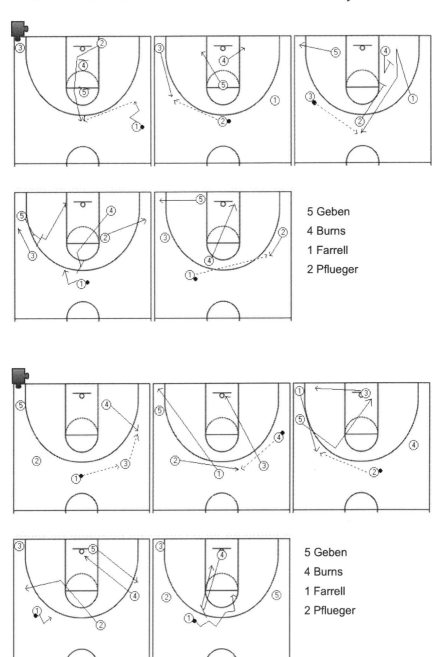

5 Geben
4 Burns
1 Farrell
2 Pflueger

5 Geben
4 Burns
1 Farrell
2 Pflueger

NCAA Basketball offense — Plays 2017-2018

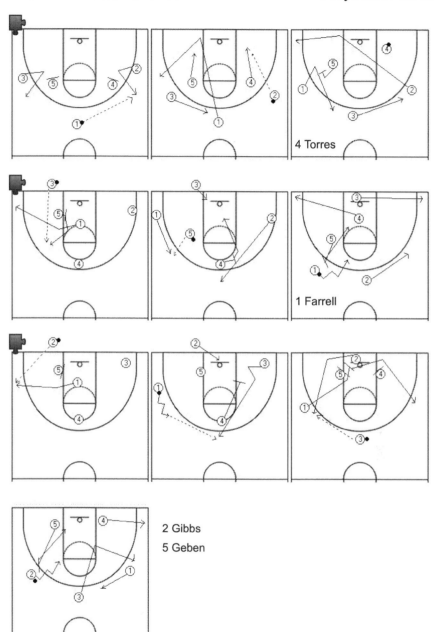

4 Torres

1 Farrell

2 Gibbs
5 Geben

Notre Dame Fighting Irish

NCAA Basketball offense — Plays 2017-2018

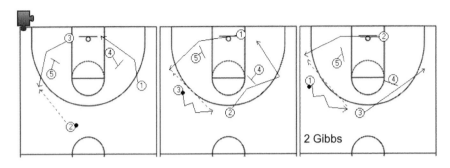

2 Gibbs

Notre Dame Fighting Irish 110

NCAA Basketball offense　　　　　　　　　　Plays 2017-2018

Big 12

OKLAHOMA SOONERS

Roster

#	Name	Position	Status
0	Christian James	Shooting Guard	Starter
1	Rashard Odomes	Small Forward	Starter
2	Chris Giles		
3	Khadeem Lattin	Power Forward	Starter
4	Jamuni McNeace	Power Forward	
5	Matt Freeman	Power Forward	
11	Trae Young	Point Guard	Starter Star
13	Jordan Sheperd	Point Guard	
14	Ty Lazenby	Small Forward	
20	Kameron McGusty		
21	Kristian Doolittle	Small Forward	
22	Patrick Geha		
30	Marshall Thorpe	Shooting Guard	
32	Read Streller		
35	Brady Manek	Power Forward	Starter
44	Hannes Polla	Center	

Head coach	Lon Kruger
A. head coach	Chris Crutchfield
Assistant coach	Carlin Hartman
Assistant coach	Kevin Kruger

111

NCAA Basketball offense — Plays 2017-2018

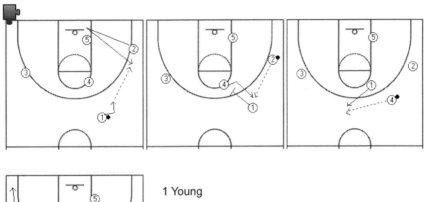

1 Young
4 Manek

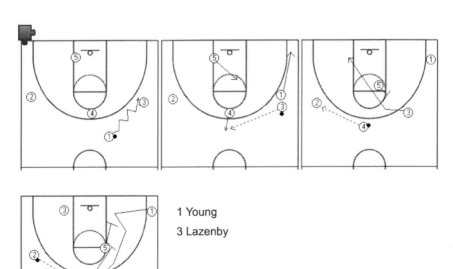

1 Young
3 Lazenby

Oklahoma Sooners

NCAA Basketball offense — Plays 2017-2018

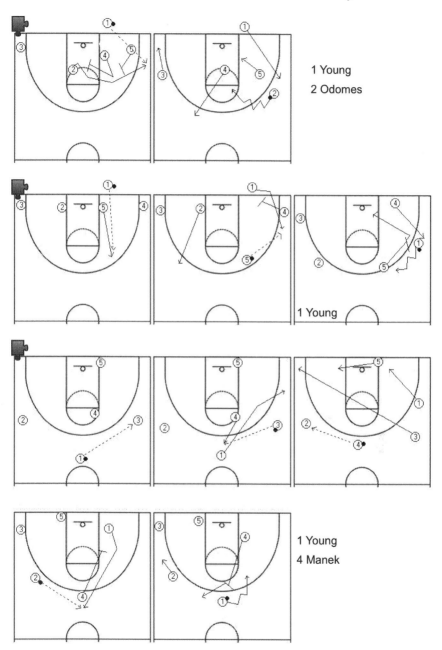

1 Young
2 Odomes

1 Young

1 Young
4 Manek

Oklahoma Sooners

NCAA Basketball offense

Plays 2017-2018

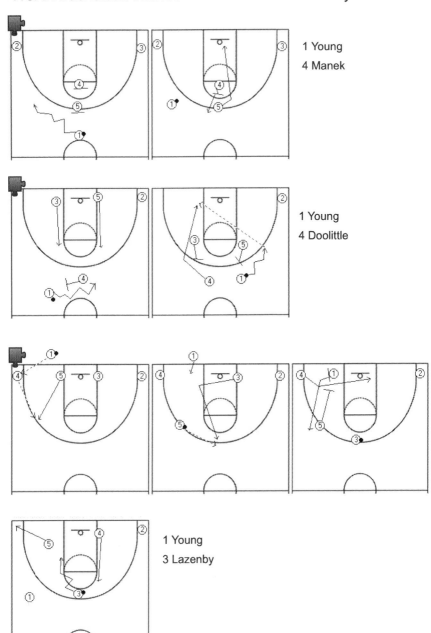

1 Young
4 Manek

1 Young
4 Doolittle

1 Young
3 Lazenby

Oklahoma Sooners

NCAA Basketball offense — Plays 2017-2018

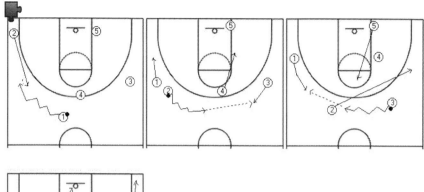

1 Young
4 Manek
5 Lattin

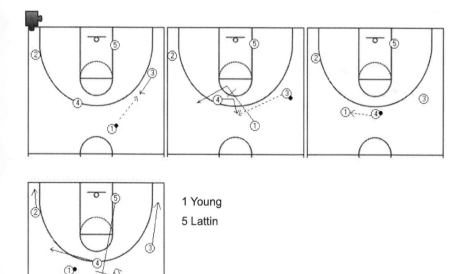

1 Young
5 Lattin

Oklahoma Sooners

NCAA Basketball offense
Plays 2017-2018

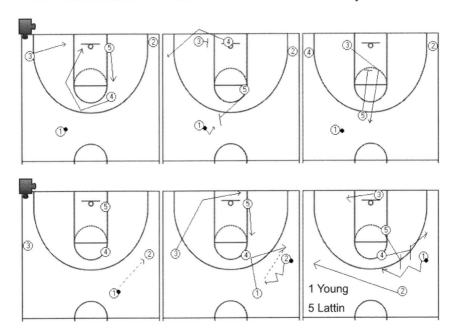

1 Young
5 Lattin

Oklahoma Sooners

NCAA Basketball offense — Plays 2017-2018

BIG Ten

PURDUE BOILERMAKERS

Roster

#	Name	Position	
1	Aaron Wheeler		
3	Carsen Edwards	Shooting Guard	Starter
5	Eden Ewing		
11	P.J. Thompson	Point Guard	Starter
12	Vicent Edwards	Power Forward	Starter
14	Ryan Cline	Shooting Guard	
15	Tommy Luce		
20	Nojel Eastern	Point Guard	
23	Jacquil Taylor		
24	Grady Eifert		
31	Dakota Mathias	Small Forward	Starter
32	Matt Haarms	Center	
44	Isaac Haas	Center	Starter Star
55	Sasha Stefanovic		

Head coach	Matt Painter
Assistant coach	Steve Lutz
Assistant coach	Greg Gary
Assistant coach	Brandon Brantley

NCAA Basketball offense — Plays 2017-2018

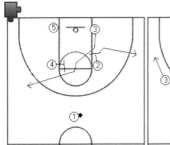

2 C. Edwards
5 Haas
1 Thompson

2 C. Edwards
5 Haas
1 Thompson

Purdue Boilermakers

NCAA Basketball offense   Plays 2017-2018

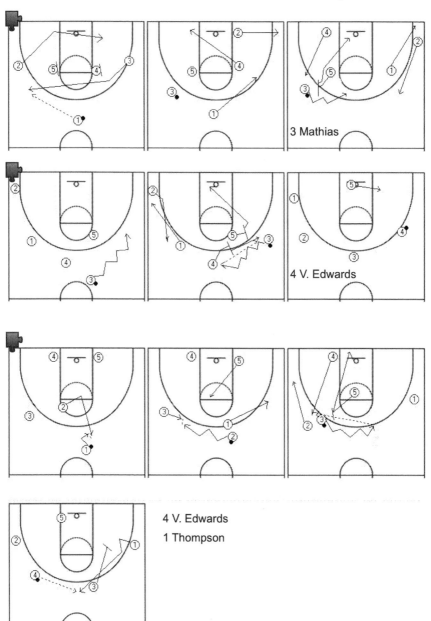

3 Mathias

4 V. Edwards

4 V. Edwards
1 Thompson

Purdue Boilermakers

NCAA Basketball offense — Plays 2017-2018

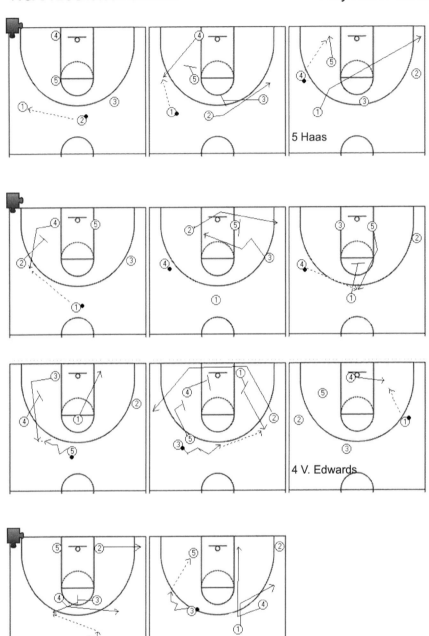

5 Haas

4 V. Edwards

5 Haas

Purdue Boilermakers

NCAA Basketball offense — Plays 2017-2018

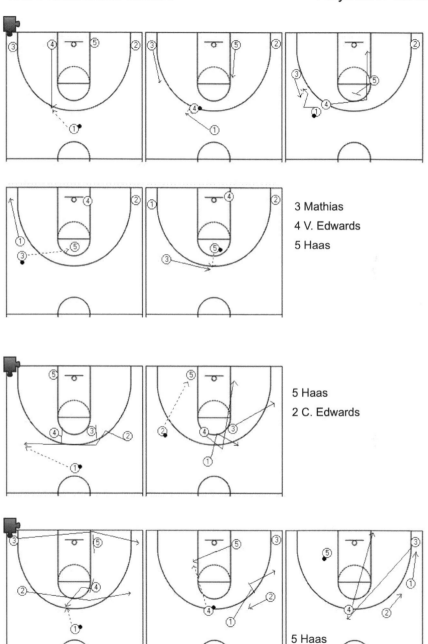

3 Mathias
4 V. Edwards
5 Haas

5 Haas
2 C. Edwards

5 Haas

Purdue Boilermakers

NCAA Basketball offense   Plays 2017-2018

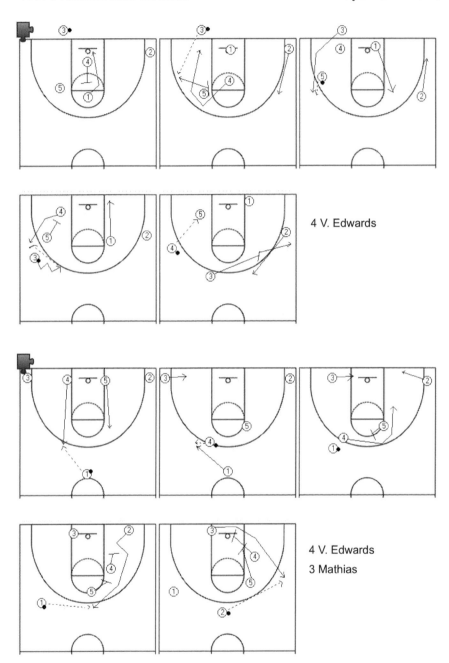

4 V. Edwards

4 V. Edwards
3 Mathias

Purdue Boilermakers   122

NCAA Basketball offense　　　　Plays 2017-2018

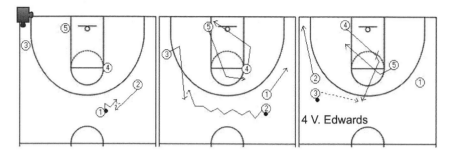

4 V. Edwards

Purdue Boilermakers

NCAA Basketball offense — Plays 2017-2018

BIG East Conference

SETON HALL PIRATES

Roster

#	Name	Position	
0	Khadeen Carrington	Point Guard	Starter
1	Michael Nzei	Power Forward	
2	Jordan Walker	Point Guard	
4	Eron Gordon		
13	Myles Powell	Small Forward	Starter
14	Ismael Sanogo	Power Forward	Starter
20	Desi Rodriguez	Shooting Guard	Starter
21	Shavar Reynolds		
22	Myles Cale	Small Forward	
23	Sandro Mamukelashvili	Center	
25	Philip Flory	Small Forward	
30	Quincy McKnight		
31	Angel Delgado	Center	Starter
33	Taurean Thompson		
35	Romaro Gill	Center	

Head coach — Kevin Willard
A. Head coach — Shaheen Holloway
Assistant coach — Fred Hill
Assistant coach — Grant Billmeier

NCAA Basketball offense — Plays 2017-2018

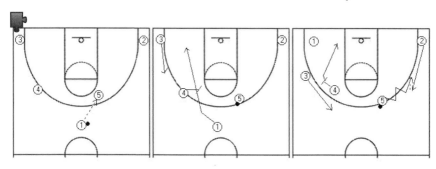

2 Rodriguez
5 Delgado
1 Carrington

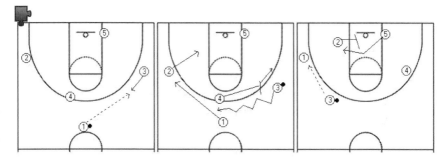

2 Rodriguez
5 Delgado
1 Carrington

Seton Hall Pirates

NCAA Basketball offense — Plays 2017-2018

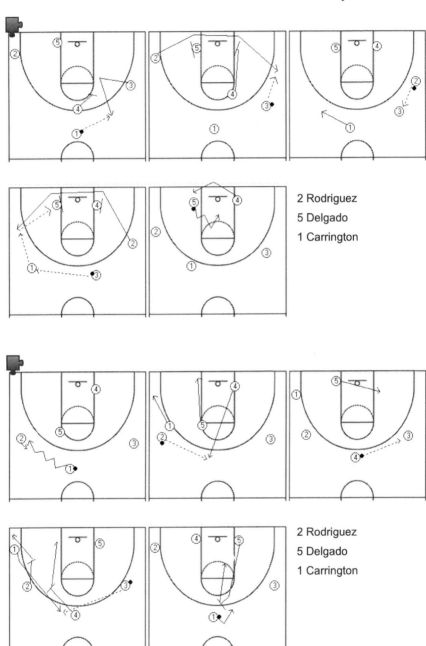

2 Rodriguez
5 Delgado
1 Carrington

Seton Hall Pirates

NCAA Basketball offense   Plays 2017-2018

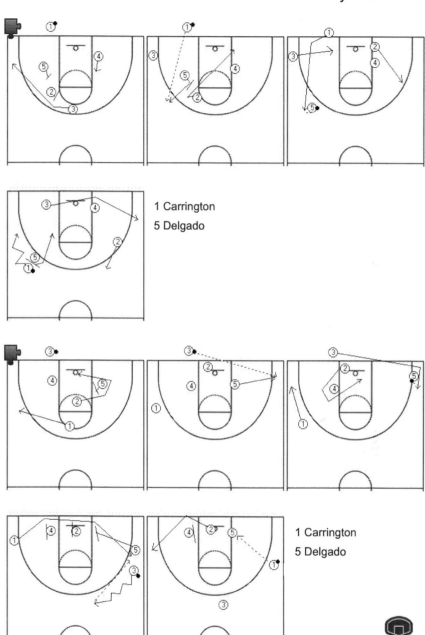

1 Carrington
5 Delgado

1 Carrington
5 Delgado

Seton Hall Pirates   127

NCAA Basketball offense

Plays 2017-2018

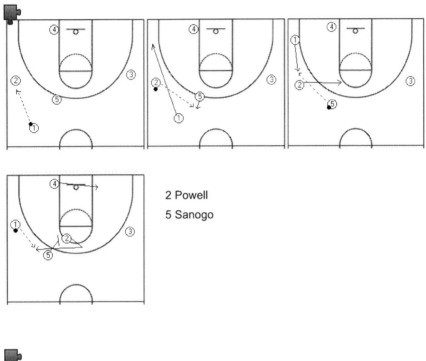

2 Powell
5 Sanogo

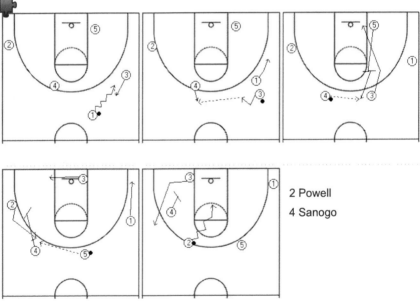

2 Powell
4 Sanogo

Seton Hall Pirates

NCAA Basketball offense   Plays 2017-2018

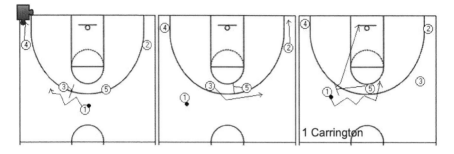

1 Carrington

Seton Hall Pirates   129

NCAA Basketball offense   Plays 2017-2018

BIG 12

TCU HORNED FROGS

Roster

0	Jaylen Fisher	Point Guard	Starter
1	Desmond Bane	Shooting Guard	Starter
2	Shawn Olden		
10	Vladimir Brodziansky	Power Forward	Starter Star
12	Kouat Noi	Power Forward	
13	Lat Mayen		
15	JD Miller	Power Forward	Starter
20	Dalton Dry		
21	Kevin Samuel	Center	
22	RJ Nembhard		
23	Ahmed Hamdy	Center	
25	Alex Robinson	Point Guard	
33	Clayton Crawford		
34	Kenrich Williams	Small Forward	Starter
45	Austin Sottile		

Head coach   Jamie Dixon
Assistant coach   David Patrick
Assistant coach   Ryan Miller
Assistant coach   Corey Barker
Special Assistant H. C.   Ontario Lett

NCAA Basketball offense — Plays 2017-2018

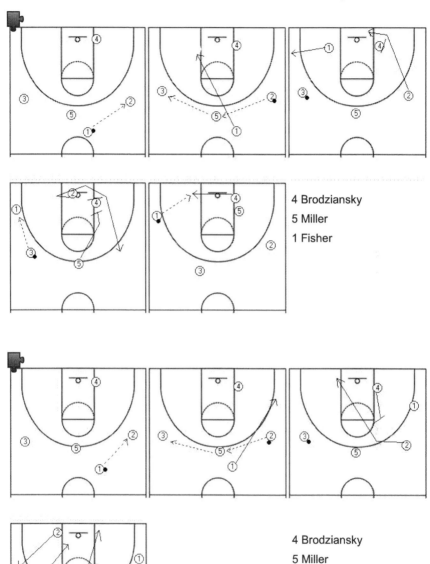

4 Brodziansky
5 Miller
1 Fisher

4 Brodziansky
5 Miller
3 Williams

TCU Horned Frogs

NCAA Basketball offense

Plays 2017-2018

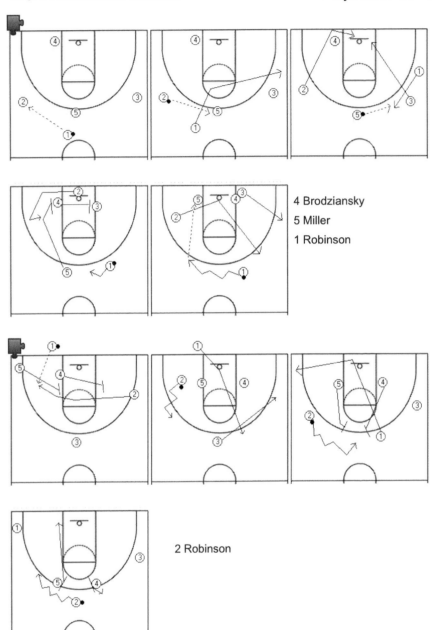

4 Brodziansky
5 Miller
1 Robinson

2 Robinson

TCU Horned Frogs

NCAA Basketball offense — Plays 2017-2018

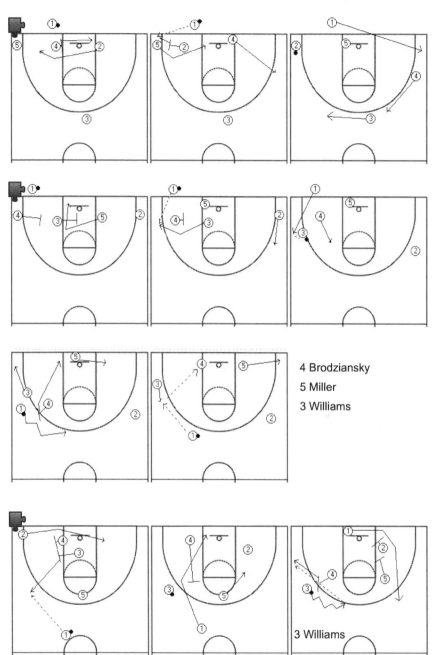

4 Brodziansky
5 Miller
3 Williams

3 Williams

TCU Horned Frogs

NCAA Basketball offense — Plays 2017-2018

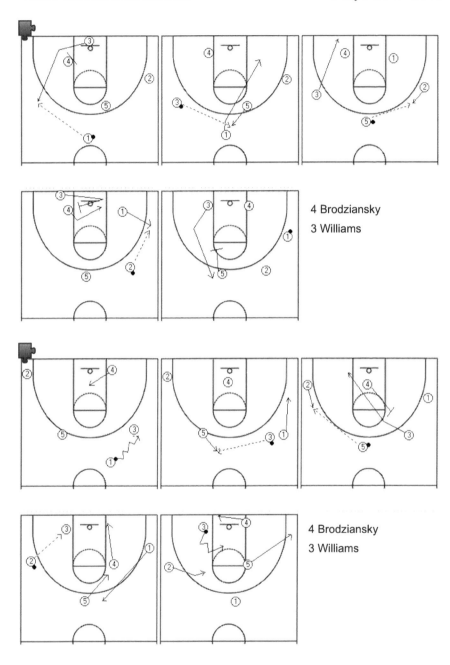

4 Brodziansky
3 Williams

4 Brodziansky
3 Williams

TCU Horned Frogs

NCAA Basketball offense   Plays 2017-2018

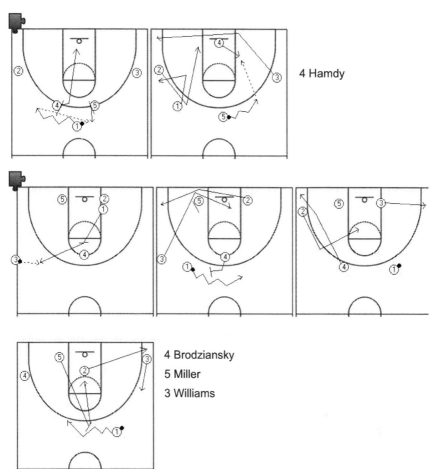

4 Hamdy

4 Brodziansky
5 Miller
3 Williams

TCU Horned Frogs

NCAA Basketball offense — Plays 2017-2018

SEC Conference

TENNESSEE VOLUNTEERS

Roster

#	Name	Position	Role
0	Jordan Bone	Point Guard	Starter
1	Lamonte Turner	Shooting Guard	
2	Grant Williams	Power Forward	Starter Star
3	James Daniel III		
4	Jacob Fleschman		
5	Admiral Schofield	Small Forward	Starter
10	John Fulkerson	Center	
11	Kyle Alexander	Power Forward	Starter
12	Brad Woodson		
13	Jalen Johnson		
15	Derrick Walker		
23	Jordan Bowden	Shooting Guard	Starter
24	Lucas Campbell		
32	Chris Darrington		
33	Zach Kent		
35	Yves Pons		

Head coach	Rick Barnes
A. Head coach	Rob Lanier
Assistant coach	Desmond Oliver
Assistant coach	Michael Schwartz
Assistant head coach	Kyle Condon

NCAA Basketball offense — Plays 2017-2018

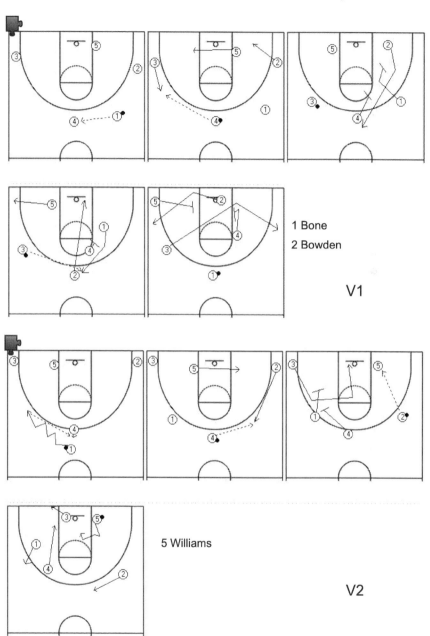

1 Bone
2 Bowden

V1

5 Williams

V2

Tennessee Volunteers

NCAA Basketball offense — Plays 2017-2018

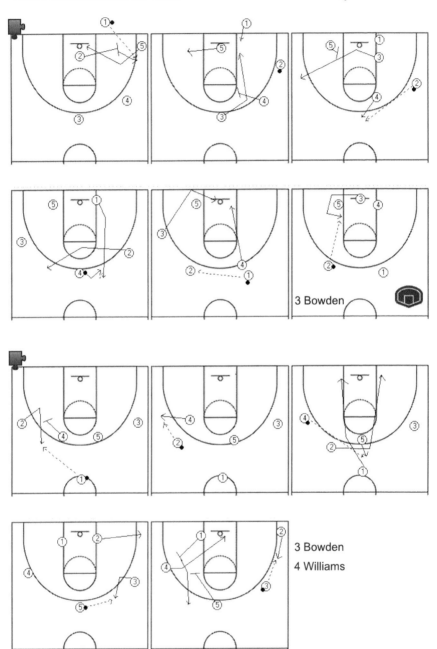

3 Bowden

3 Bowden
4 Williams

Tennessee Volunteers

NCAA Basketball offense — Plays 2017-2018

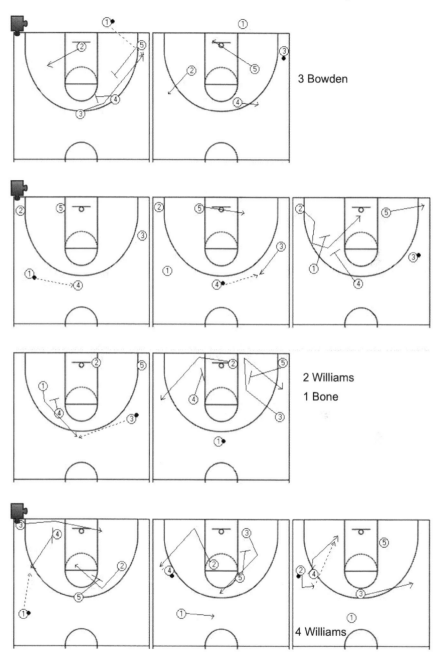

3 Bowden

2 Williams
1 Bone

4 Williams

Tennessee Volunteers

NCAA Basketball offense — Plays 2017-2018

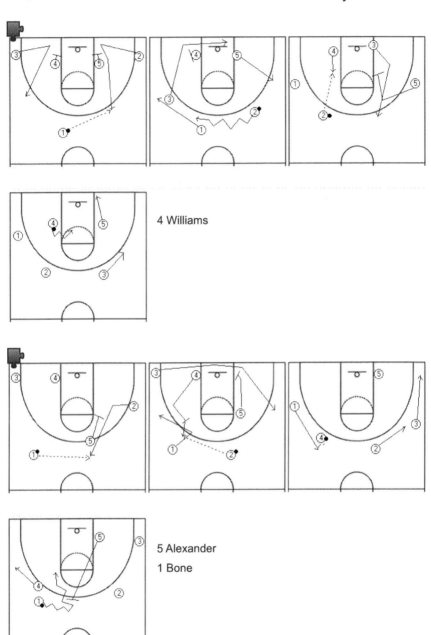

4 Williams

5 Alexander
1 Bone

Tennessee Volunteers — 140

NCAA Basketball offense Plays 2017-2018

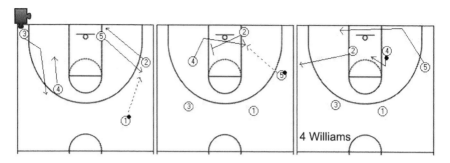

4 Williams

NCAA Basketball offense — Plays 2017-2018

SEC Conference

TEXAS A&M AGGIES

Roster

#	Name	Position	Status
0	Jay Jay Chandler		
1	DJ Hogg	Small Forward	Starter
2	TJ Starks	Shooting Guard	
3	Admon Gilder	Shotting Guard	Starter
4	JJ Caldwell	Point Guard	
5	Savion Flagg	Center	
10	Tonny Trocha-Morelos	Power Forward	
11	Mark French		
12	Chris Collins		
13	Duane Wilson	Point Guard	Starter
15	Isiah Jasey		
22	Frank Byers		
24	John Walker III		
32	Josh Nebo		
33	Cameron Alo		
34	Tyler Davis	Center	Starter
44	Robert Williams	Power Forward	Starter Star

Head coach	Billy Kennedy
Assistant coach	Amir Abdur-Rahim
Assistant coach	Isaac Chew
Assistant coach	Ulric Maligi

NCAA Basketball offense   Plays 2017-2018

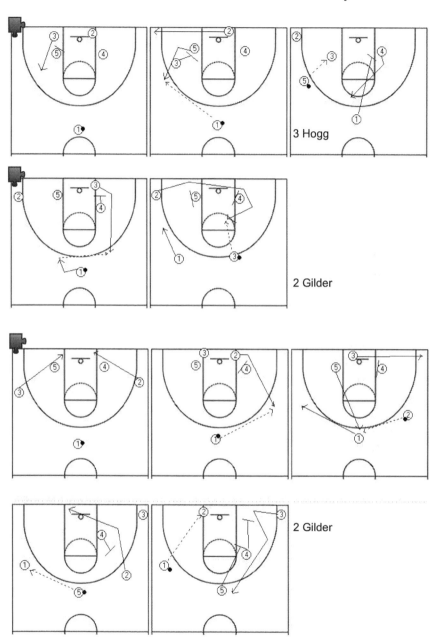

3 Hogg

2 Gilder

2 Gilder

Texas A&M Aggies

NCAA Basketball offense

Plays 2017-2018

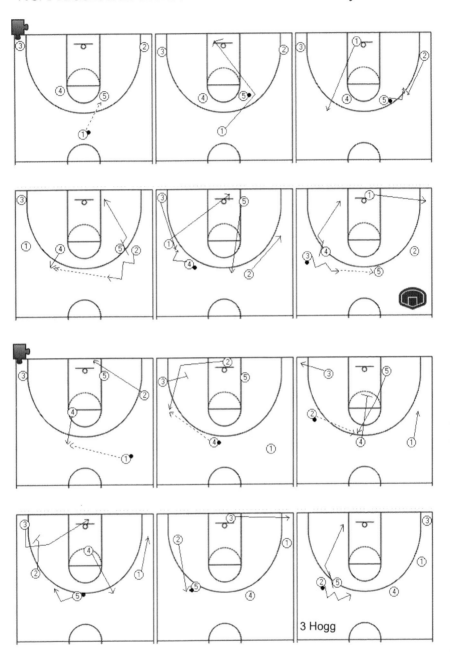

3 Hogg

Texas A&M Aggies

NCAA Basketball offense — Plays 2017-2018

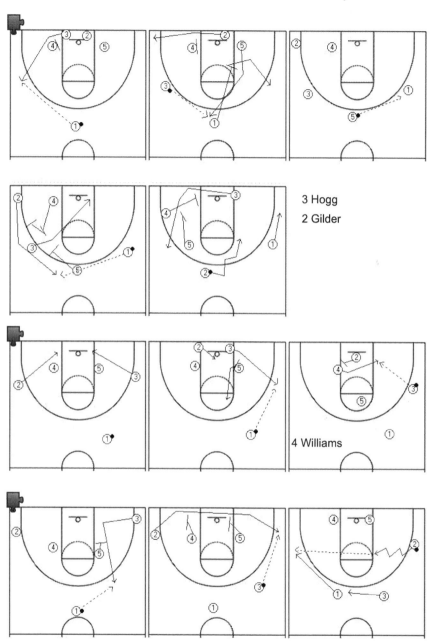

3 Hogg
2 Gilder

4 Williams

Texas A&M Aggies

NCAA Basketball offense

Plays 2017-2018

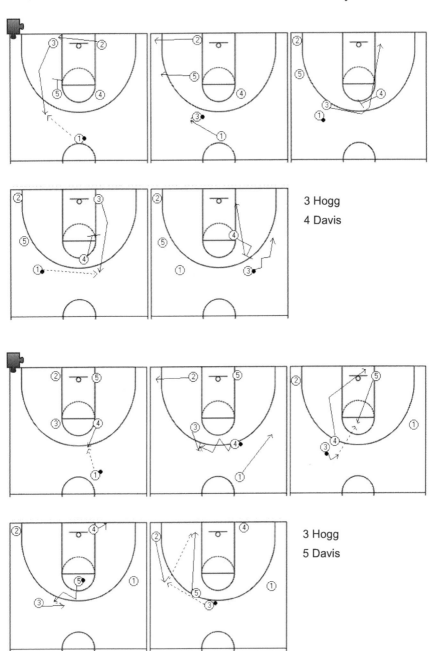

3 Hogg
4 Davis

3 Hogg
5 Davis

Texas A&M Aggies

NCAA Basketball offense — Plays 2017-2018

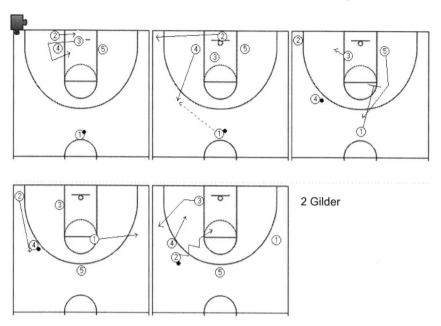

2 Gilder

NCAA Basketball offense — Plays 2017-2018

Big 12

TEXAS LONGHORNS

Roster

#	Name	Position	Status
00	James Banks III		
1	Andrew Jones	Small Forward	Starter
2	Matt Coleman	Point Guard	Starter Pass
3	Jacob Young	Shooting Guard	
4	Mohamed Bamba	Center	Starter Star
5	Royce Hamm Jr.		
10	Eric Davis Jr.	Shooting Guard	
12	Kerwin Roach II	Shooting Guard	Starter
13	Jase Febres		
20	Jericho Sims	Power Forward	
21	Dylan Osetkowski	Center	Starter
22	Isaiah Hobbs		
25	Joe Schwartz		
30	Ryan Mcclurg		
55	Elijah Mitrou-Long		

Head coach	Shaka Smart
Assistant coach	Darrin Horn
Assistant coach	Jai Lucas
Assistant coach	Mike Morrell

NCAA Basketball offense　　　　　Plays 2017-2018

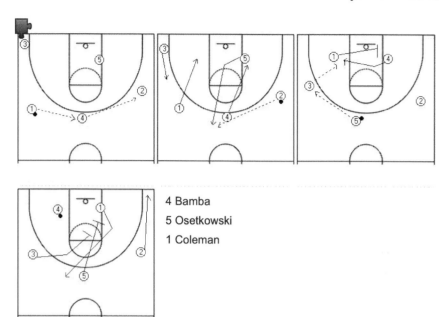

4 Bamba
5 Osetkowski
1 Coleman

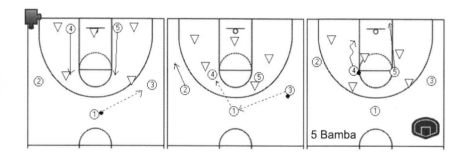

5 Bamba

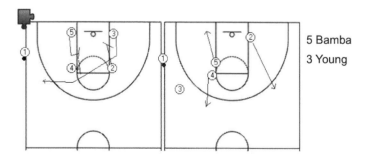

5 Bamba
3 Young

Texas Longhorns

NCAA Basketball offense   Plays 2017-2018

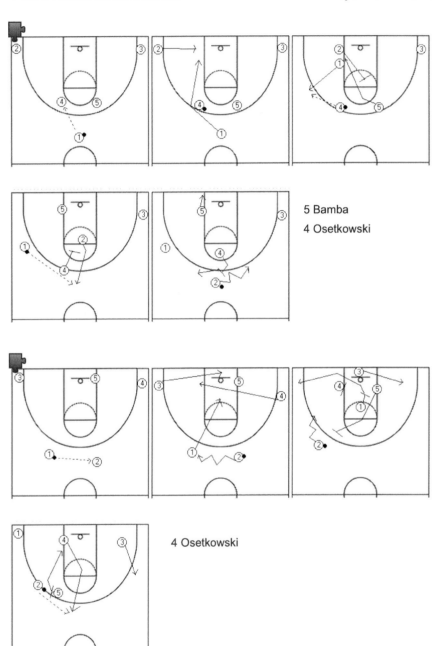

5 Bamba
4 Osetkowski

4 Osetkowski

Texas Longhorns   150

NCAA Basketball offense   Plays 2017-2018

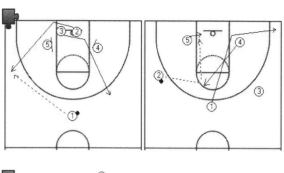

5 Bamba
4 Osetkowski

5 Bamba
4 Osetkowski

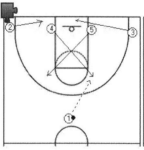  

5 Bamba
2 Roach II

Texas Longhorns

NCAA Basketball offense — Plays 2017-2018

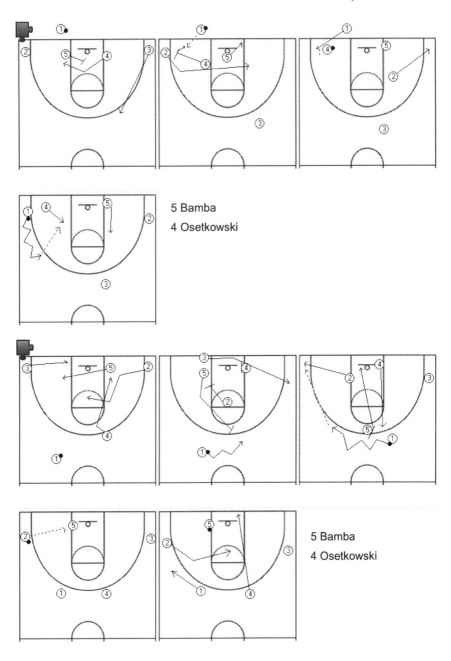

5 Bamba
4 Osetkowski

5 Bamba
4 Osetkowski

Texas Longhorns

NCAA Basketball offense — Plays 2017-2018

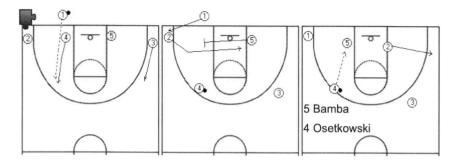

5 Bamba
4 Osetkowski

Texas Longhorns 153

NCAA Basketball offense — Plays 2017-2018

BIG 12

TEXAS TECH RED RAIDERS

Roster

#	Name	Position	Status
0	Tommy Hamilton IV	Center	
1	Brandone Francis	Point Guard	
2	Zhaire Smith	Power Forward	Starter
3	Josh Webster		
5	Justin Gray	Shooting Guard	Starter
10	Niem Stevenson	Small Forward	Starter
11	Zach Smith		
12	Keenan Evans	Point Guard	Starter
21	Malik Ondigo		
23	Jarrett Culver	Shooting Guard	
24	Avery Benson		
25	Davide Moretti	Small Forward	
30	Andrew Sorrells		
32	Norense Odiase	Center	Starter
35	Parker Hicks		

Head coach	Chris Beard
Assistant coach	Mark Adams
Assistant coach	Chris Ogden
Assistant coach	Al Pinkins

NCAA Basketball offense   Plays 2017-2018

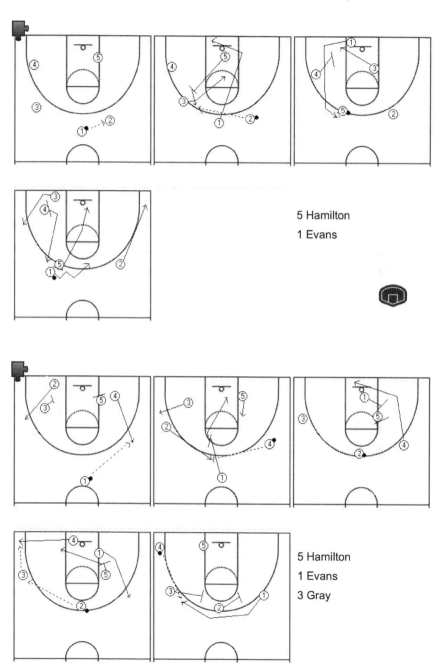

5 Hamilton
1 Evans

5 Hamilton
1 Evans
3 Gray

Texas Tech Red Raiders   155

NCAA Basketball offense — Plays 2017-2018

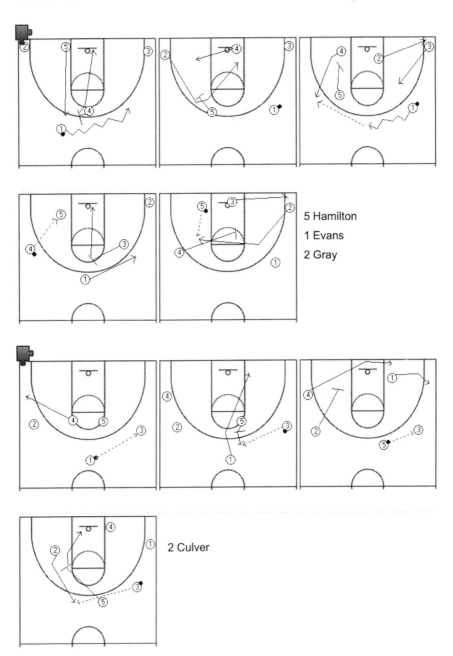

5 Hamilton
1 Evans
2 Gray

2 Culver

Texas Tech Red Raiders

NCAA Basketball offense Plays 2017-2018

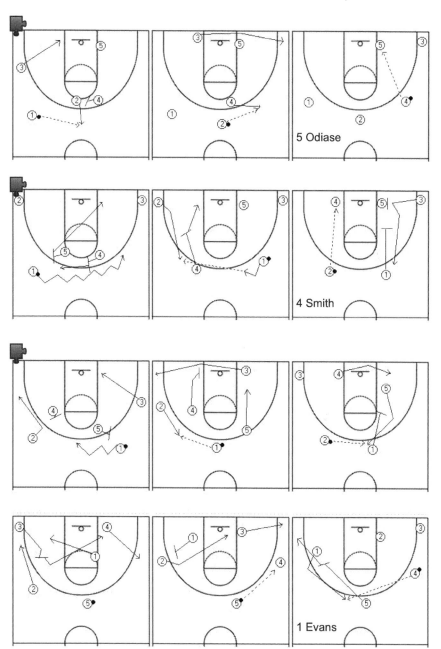

5 Odiase

4 Smith

1 Evans

Texas Tech Red Raiders 157

NCAA Basketball offense

Plays 2017-2018

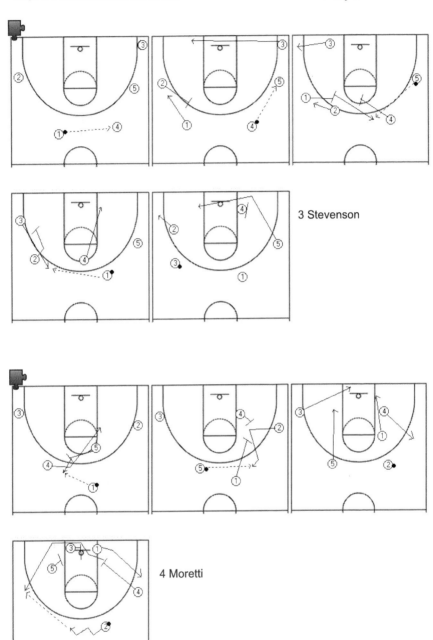

3 Stevenson

4 Moretti

Texas Tech Red Raiders

NCAA Basketball offense — Plays 2017-2018

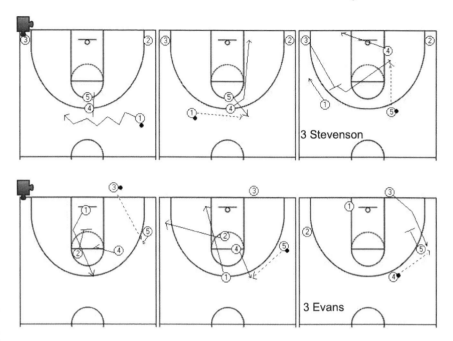

3 Stevenson

3 Evans

Texas Tech Red Raiders

NCAA Basketball offense — Plays 2017-2018

PAC - 12

UCLA BRUINS

Roster

#	Name	Position	Role
0	Alex Olesinski	Center	
2	Cody Riley		
3	Aaron Holiday	Point Guard	Starter Scorer
4	Jaylen Hands	Shooting Guard	Star
5	Chris Smith	Power Forward	
10	Isaac Wulff		
13	Kris Wilkes	Small Forward	Starter
14	Gyorgy Goloman	Center	Starter
15	LiAngelo Ball (preseason)		
21	Alec Wulff		
22	Armani Dodson		
23	Prince Ali	Small Forward	Starter
24	Jalen Hill		
30	Joseph Wallace		
34	Ikenna Okwarabizie		
40	Thomas Welsh	Power Forward	Starter Star

Head coach — Steve Alford
Associate h. coach — Duane Broussard
Assistant coach — David Grace
Assistant coach — Tyus Edney

NCAA Basketball offense — Plays 2017-2018

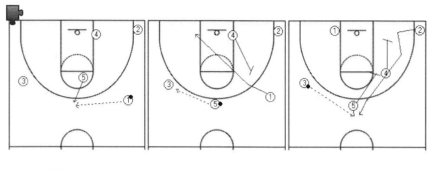

4 Welsh
5 Goloman
1 Holiday
3 Ali

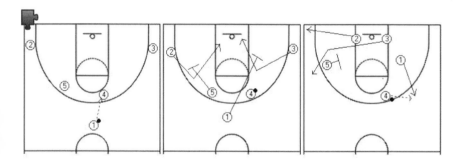

4 Welsh
5 Goloman
1 Hands

Ucla Bruins

NCAA Basketball offense — Plays 2017-2018

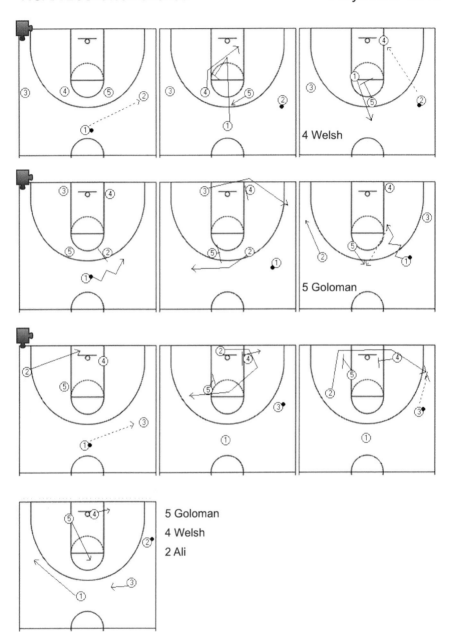

4 Welsh

5 Goloman

5 Goloman
4 Welsh
2 Ali

Ucla Bruins

NCAA Basketball offense   Plays 2017-2018

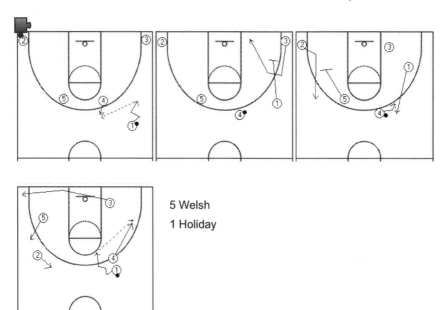

5 Welsh
1 Holiday

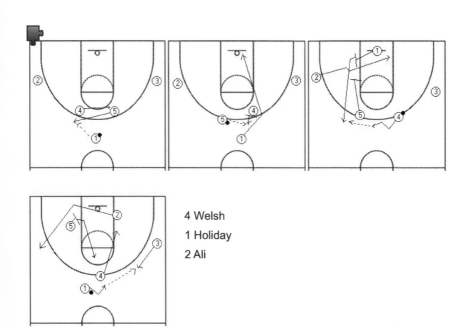

4 Welsh
1 Holiday
2 Ali

Ucla Bruins

NCAA Basketball offense — Plays 2017-2018

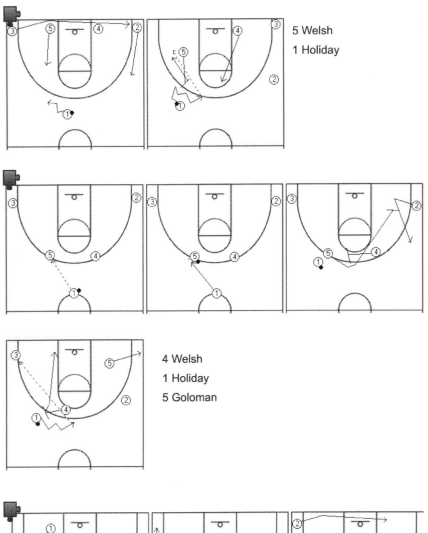

5 Welsh
1 Holiday

4 Welsh
1 Holiday
5 Goloman

4 Olesinski

Ucla Bruins

NCAA Basketball offense   Plays 2017-2018

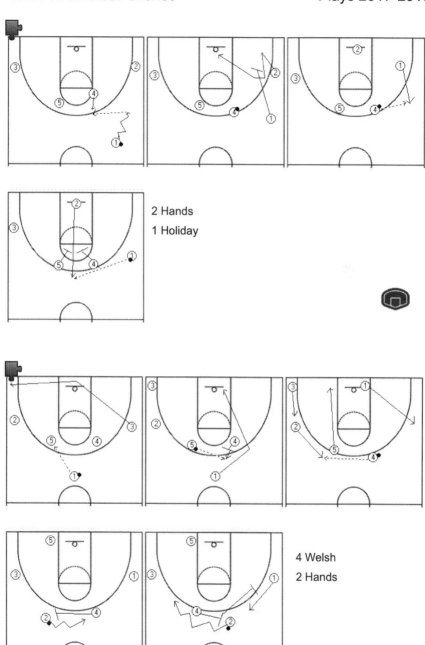

2 Hands
1 Holiday

4 Welsh
2 Hands

Ucla Bruins   165

NCAA Basketball offense — Plays 2017-2018

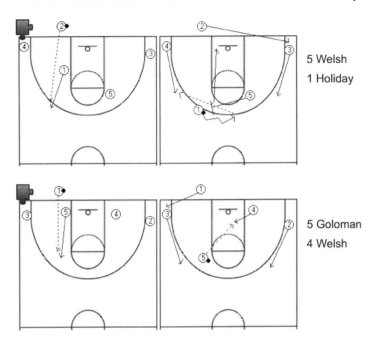

5 Welsh
1 Holiday

5 Goloman
4 Welsh

NCAA Basketball offense　　　　　　　　Plays 2017-2018

Big East Conference

VILLANOVA WILDCATS

Roster

#	Name	Position	Role
1	Jalen Brunson	Point Guard	Starter Star
2	Collin Gillespie	Shooting Guard	
4	Eric Paschall	Power Forward	Starter
5	Phil Booth	Shooting Guard	Starter
10	Donte DiVincenzo	Shooting Guard	
14	Omari Spellman	Power Forward	Starter
21	Dhamir Cosby-Roundtree	Power Forward	
22	Peyton Heck		
23	Jermaine Samuels		
24	Tom Leibig		
25	Mikal Bridges	Small Forward	Starter Star
34	Tim Delaney		
35	Matt Kennedy		
40	Denny Grace		
42	Dylan Painter		

Head coach	Jay Wright
Assistant coach	Ashley Howard
Assistant coach	Kyle Neptune
Assistant coach	George Halcovage

NCAA Basketball offense　　　Plays 2017-2018

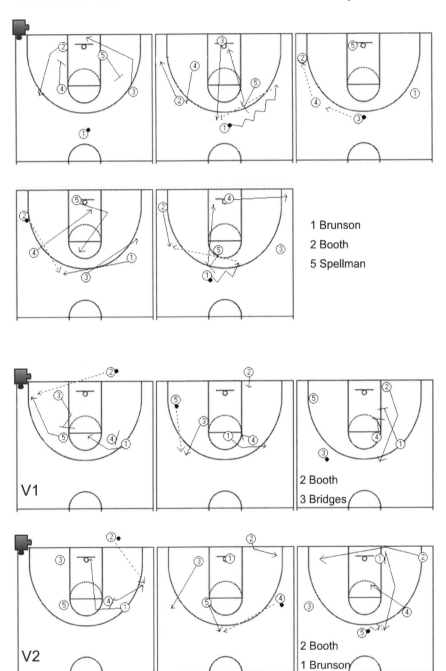

1 Brunson
2 Booth
5 Spellman

V1

V2

2 Booth
3 Bridges

2 Booth
1 Brunson

Villanova Wildcats　　　168

NCAA Basketball offense — Plays 2017-2018

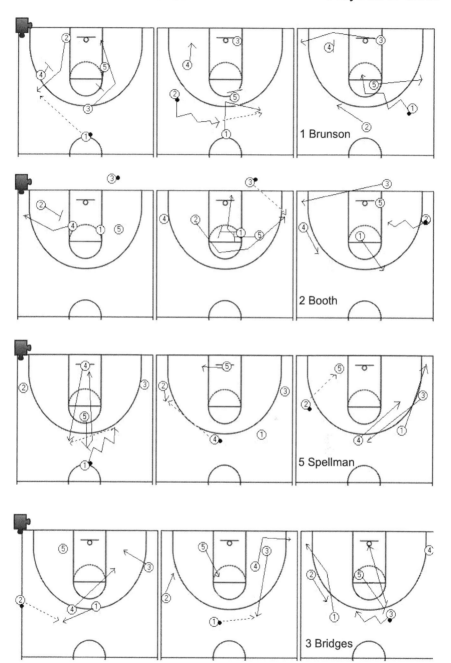

1 Brunson
2 Booth
5 Spellman
3 Bridges

Villanova Wildcats

NCAA Basketball offense — Plays 2017-2018

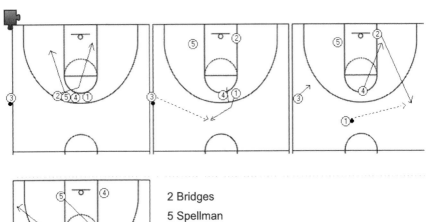

2 Bridges
5 Spellman

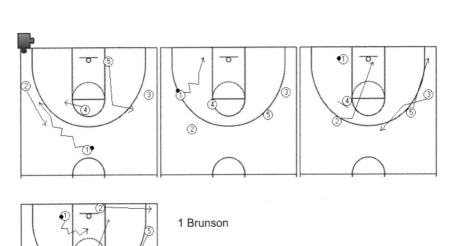

1 Brunson

Villanova Wildcats

NCAA Basketball offense — Plays 2017-2018

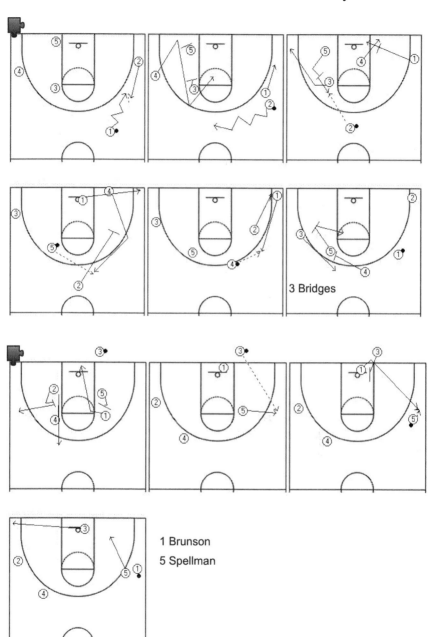

3 Bridges

1 Brunson
5 Spellman

Villanova Wildcats

NCAA Basketball offense Plays 2017-2018

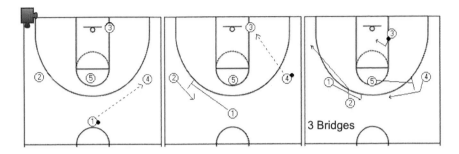

3 Bridges

Villanova Wildcats

NCAA Basketball offense — Plays 2017-2018

Atlantic Coast Conference

VIRGINIA CAVALIERS

Roster

#	Name	Position	Role
0	Devon Hall	Small Forward	Starter
1	Francesco Badocchi		
2	Justice Bartley		
5	Kyle Guy	Shooting Guard	Starter
10	Trevon Gross Jr.		
11	Ty Jerome	Point Guard	Starter
12	De'Andre Hunter	Small Forward	Starter
21	Isaiah Wilkins	Power Forward	Starter Star
23	Nigel Johnson	Point Guard	
24	Marco Anthony		
25	Mamadi Diakite	Center	
30	Jay Huff		
33	Jack Salt	Center	Starter
45	Austin Katstra		

Head coach — Tony Bennett
A. head coach — Ron Sánchez
Assistant coach — Jason Williford
Assistant coach — Brad Soderberg

NCAA Basketball offense — Plays 2017-2018

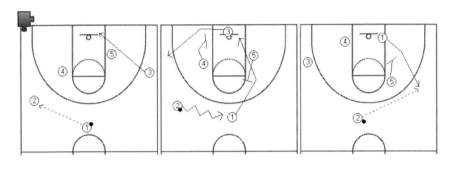

5 Salt

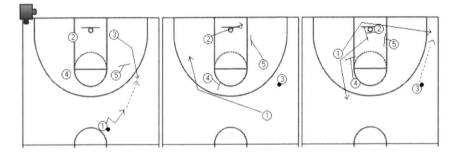

1 Jerome
5 Salt

Virginia Cavaliers

NCAA Basketball offense

Plays 2017-2018

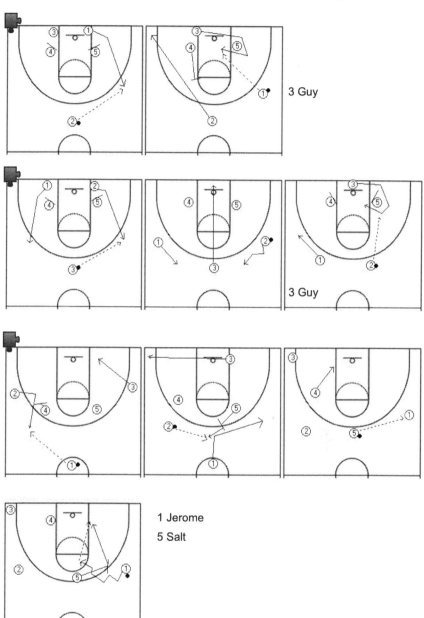

3 Guy

3 Guy

1 Jerome
5 Salt

Virginia Cavaliers

NCAA Basketball offense
Plays 2017-2018

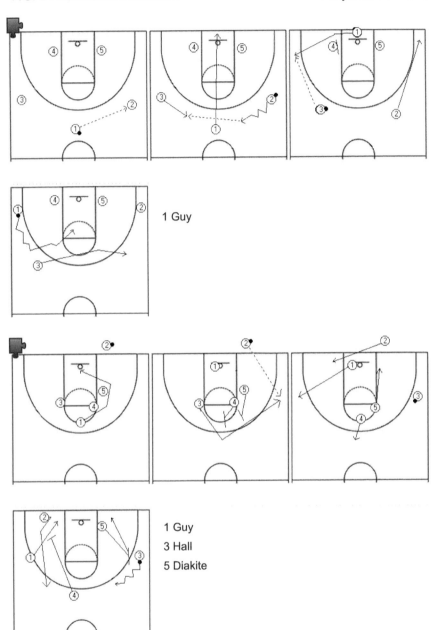

1 Guy

1 Guy
3 Hall
5 Diakite

Virginia Cavaliers

NCAA Basketball offense

Plays 2017-2018

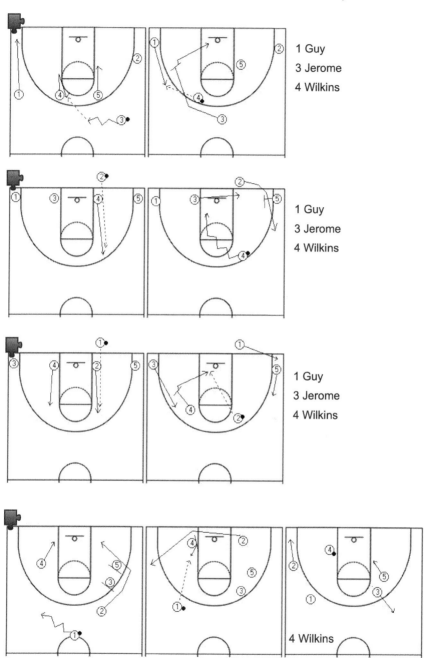

1 Guy
3 Jerome
4 Wilkins

1 Guy
3 Jerome
4 Wilkins

1 Guy
3 Jerome
4 Wilkins

4 Wilkins

Virginia Cavaliers 177

NCAA Basketball offense — Plays 2017-2018

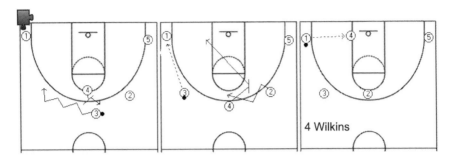

4 Wilkins

Virginia Cavaliers

NCAA Basketball offense Plays 2017-2018

Big 12 Conference

WEST VIRGINIA MOUNTAINEERS

Roster

#	Name	Position	Role
2	Jevon Carter	Point Guard	Starter Star
3	James Bolden	Shooting Guard	
4	Daxter Miles Jr.	Shooting Guard	Starter
5	Brandon Knapper		
11	D'Angelo Hunter		
13	Teddy Allen	Power Forward	
14	Chase Harler	Small Forward	
15	Lamont West	Small Forward	Starter
21	Wesley Harris	Small Forward	Starter
23	Esa Ahmad		
25	Maciej Bender	Center	
31	Logan Routt		
50	Sagaba Konate	Center	Starter

Head coach	Bob Huggins
A. head coach	Larry Harrison
Assistant coach	Ron Everhart
Assistant coach	Erik Martin

NCAA Basketball offense

Plays 2017-2018

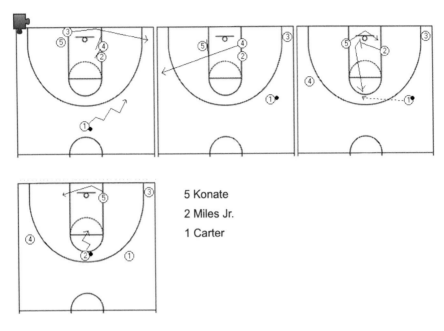

5 Konate
2 Miles Jr.
1 Carter

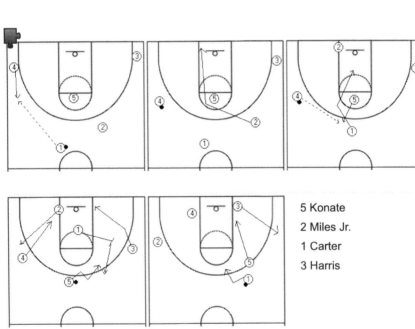

5 Konate
2 Miles Jr.
1 Carter
3 Harris

West Virginia Mountaineers

NCAA Basketball offense   Plays 2017-2018

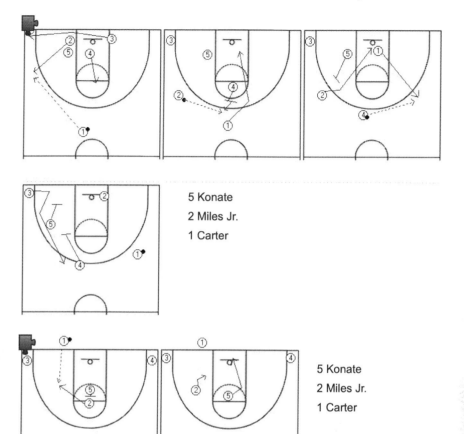

5 Konate
2 Miles Jr.
1 Carter

5 Konate
2 Miles Jr.
1 Carter

5 Allen

West Virginia Mountaineers

NCAA Basketball offense   Plays 2017-2018

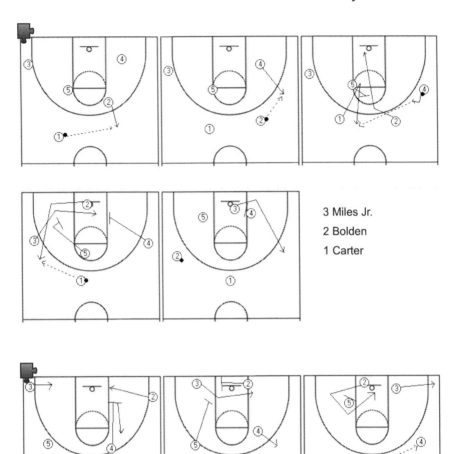

3 Miles Jr.
2 Bolden
1 Carter

5 Konate
2 Miles Jr.
1 Carter
3 Harris

West Virginia Mountaineers

NCAA Basketball offense — Plays 2017-2018

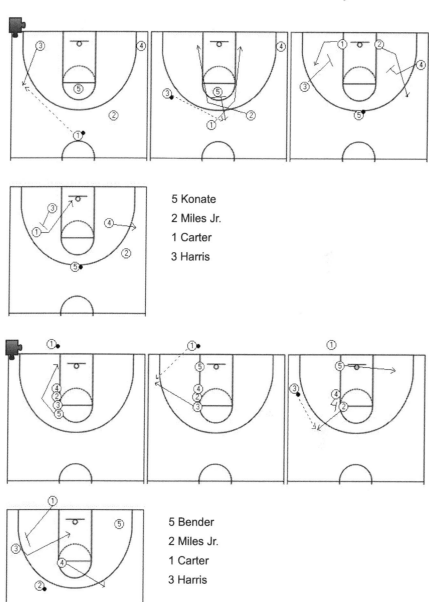

5 Konate
2 Miles Jr.
1 Carter
3 Harris

5 Bender
2 Miles Jr.
1 Carter
3 Harris

West Virginia Mountaineers

NCAA Basketball offense — Plays 2017-2018

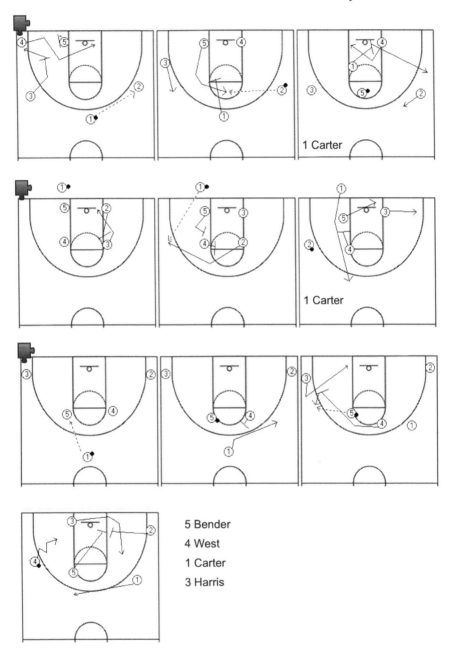

1 Carter

1 Carter

5 Bender
4 West
1 Carter
3 Harris

West Virginia Mountaineers

NCAA Basketball offense — Plays 2017-2018

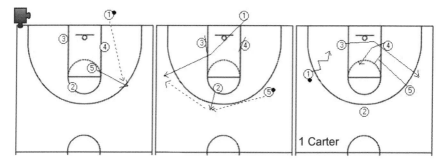

1 Carter

West Virginia Mountaineers

NCAA Basketball offense — Plays 2017-2018

American Athletic Conference

WICHITA STATE SHOCKERS

Roster

#	Name	Position	Role
0	Rashard Kelly	Power Forward	Starter
1	Zach Brown	Small Forward	Starter
3	C.J. Keyser		
4	Samajae Haynes-Jones		
5	Rod Brown		
10	Kaelen Malone		
11	Landry Shamet	Point Guard	Starter Star
12	Austin Reaves	Shooting Guard	
14	Jacob Herrs		
20	Rauno Nuger	Power Forward	
21	Darral Willis Jr.	Center	
22	Asbjørn Midtgaard		
23	Brycen Bush		
24	Shaquille Morris	Center	Starter
25	Brett Barney		
32	Markis McDuffie		
33	Conner Frankamp	Shooting Guard	Starter

Head coach	Gregg Marshall
Assistant coach	Isaac Brown
Assistant coach	Kyle Lindsted
Assistant coach	Donnie Jones

NCAA Basketball offense — Plays 2017-2018

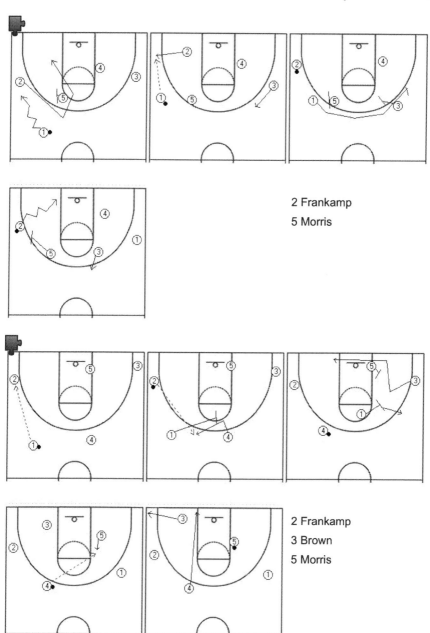

2 Frankamp
5 Morris

2 Frankamp
3 Brown
5 Morris

Wichita State Shockers

NCAA Basketball offense — Plays 2017-2018

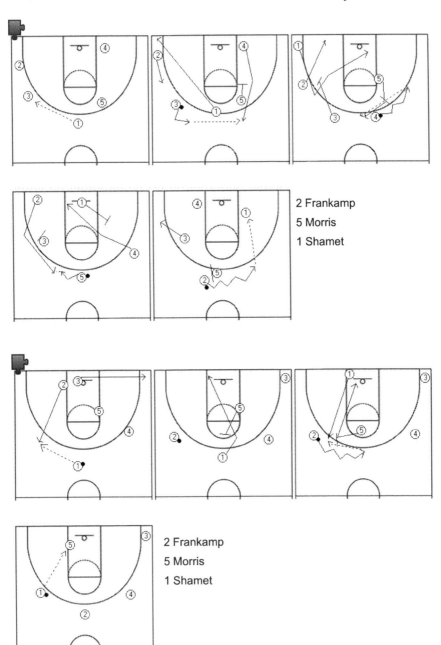

2 Frankamp
5 Morris
1 Shamet

Wichita State Shockers

NCAA Basketball offense — Plays 2017-2018

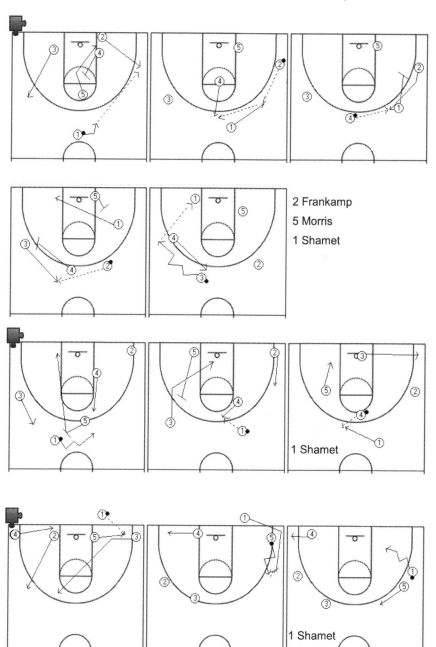

2 Frankamp
5 Morris
1 Shamet

1 Shamet

1 Shamet

Wichita State Shockers

NCAA Basketball offense   Plays 2017-2018

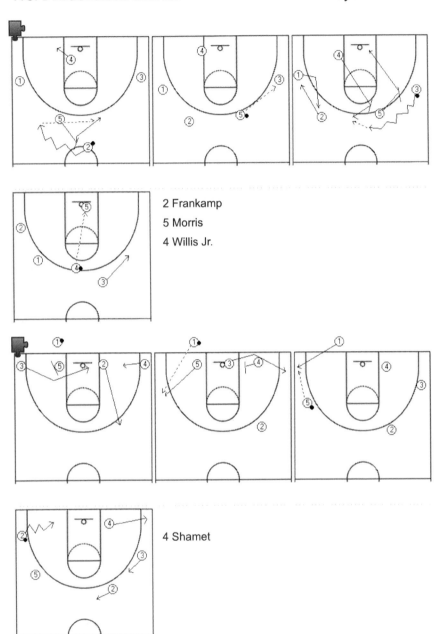

2 Frankamp
5 Morris
4 Willis Jr.

4 Shamet

Wichita State Shockers

NCAA Basketball offense Plays 2017-2018

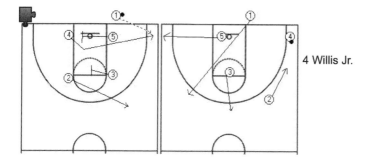

4 Willis Jr.

Wichita State Shockers

NCAA Basketball offense　　　　　　　　　Plays 2017-2018

Big East Conference

XAVIER MUSKETEERS

Roster

0	Tyrique Jones	Center	Starter
1	Paul Scruggs	Point Guard	
3	Quentin Goodin	Point Guard	Starter
4	Elias Harden		
5	Trevon Bluiett	Shooting Guard	Starter Star
10	Leighton Schrand		
11	Kerem Kanter	Power Forward	
12	Nick Vanderpohl	Point Guard	
13	Naji Marshall	Small Forward	
20	Matt Singleton		
22	Kaiser Gates	Power Forward	Starter
54	Sean O´Mara	Center	
55	J. P. Macura	Small Forward	Starter

Head coach	Chris Mack
A. Head coach	Travis Steele
Assistant coach	Luke Murray
Assistant coach	Mike Pegues

NCAA Basketball offense — Plays 2017-2018

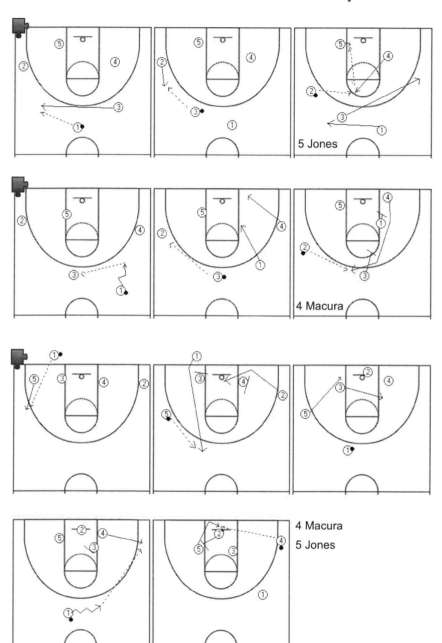

5 Jones

4 Macura

4 Macura
5 Jones

Xavier Musketeers

NCAA Basketball offense — Plays 2017-2018

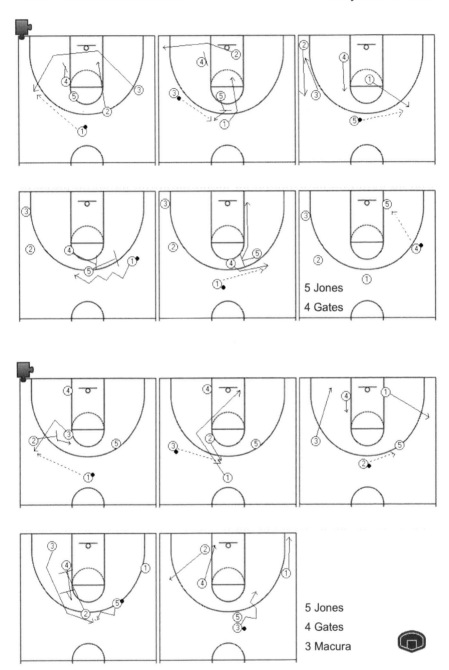

5 Jones
4 Gates
3 Macura

Xavier Musketeers

NCAA Basketball offense — Plays 2017-2018

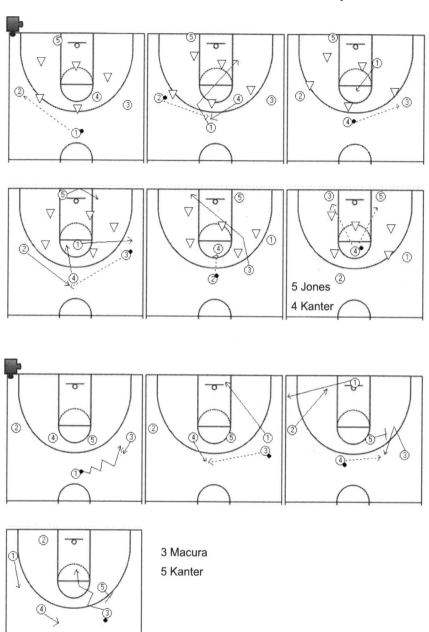

5 Jones
4 Kanter

3 Macura
5 Kanter

Xavier Musketeers

NCAA Basketball offense — Plays 2017-2018

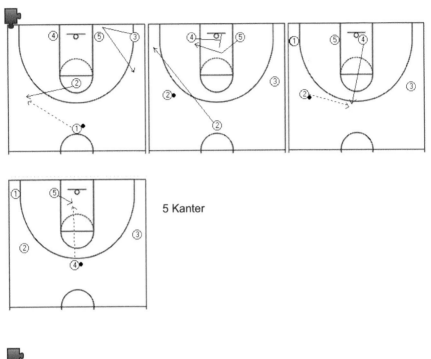

5 Kanter

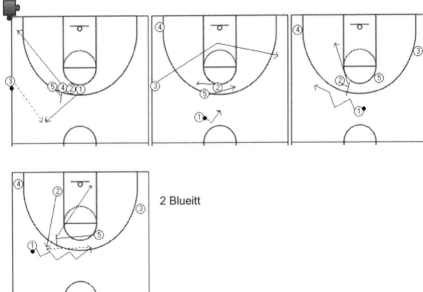

2 Blueitt

Xavier Musketeers

NCAA Basketball offense   Plays 2017-2018

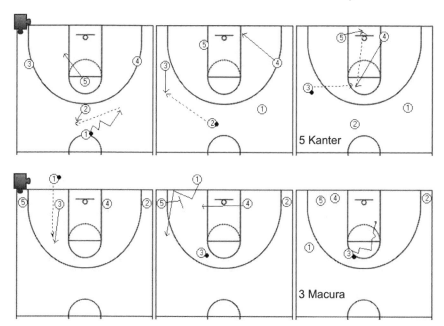

5 Kanter

3 Macura

Xavier Musketeers

NCAA Basketball offense   Plays 2017-2018

Index plays   (First number page, second, position)

Against

   Man to man

      For ball inside

         9.2 11.2 11.3 12.1 16.1 17.1 18.3 19.1 19.4 20.1
         29.2 29.3 30.2 30.3 32.1 33.2 35.1 35.3 36.1 41.2
         42.1 43.1 44.1 45.1 45.2 49.1 56.2 61.2 67.1 80.1
         87.2 92.2 94.2 97.1 97.2 99.1 101.2 107.2 109.1
         120.1 120.2 120.3 121.2 121.3 126.1 131.1 132.1
         134.2 135.1 137.2 138.2 140.1 141.1 143.1 143.3
         145.2 146.2 151.1 152.2 157.1 157.2 158.1 159.1
         162.1 169.3 170.2 172.1 177.4 178.1 181.3 187.2
         188.1 188.2 189.1 190.1 193.1 194.1 196.1 197.1

      Pick and roll

         9.1 11.1 16.3 18.1 22.1 22.2 23.1 26.1 26.2 27.1
         30.1 32.4 35.2 37.2 38.1 38.2 38.3 41.1 42.3 43.2
         48.2 48.3 49.3 50.1 50.3 51.3 53.3 54.1 54.2 56.1
         60.1 62.2 64.2 70.1 70.4 73.2 73.3 74.1 75.1 77.2
         79.1 80.2 82.1 82.2 83.1 83.2 85.2 86.1 87.1 90.1
         94.1 94.3 96.1 96.2 108.2 112.1 113.3 115.1 115.2
         116.2 119.1 119.2 121.1 125.1 126.2 129.1 131.2
         133.4 139.3 140.2 144.1 144.2 146.1 150.1 151.3
         155.1 161.2 163.1 164.1 164.2 165.2 168.1 169.4
         174.1 175.3 189.2 194.2 195.2

Index

NCAA Basketball offense   Plays 2017-2018

Cut

12.2 13.2 44.3 64.1 68.2 69.1 70.2 70.3 71.1 76.3
77.1 86.3 92.1 99.2 106.2 114.2 118.1 143.2 145.1
175.1 175.2

Final 1x1

9.3 10.2 24.2 29.4 50.2 51.1 51.2 57.2 58.1 68.1
68.3 74.2 75.2 81.1 81.3 93.2 95.1 95.2 95.3 101.1
103.1 106.1 107.1 107.3 108.1 114.1 125.2 128.2
134.1 145.3 147.1 159.2 162.2 163.2 164.3 169.1
174.2 176.1 180.1 180.2 184.1 184.3 187.1

Shooters

10.3 25.2 31.2 32.3 69.3 85.1 88.2 89.1 89.2 93.1
99.3 100.1 102.1 103.2 109.4 112.2 116.1 118.2
119.3 122.2 123.1 128.1 137.1 139.2 149.1 150.2
155.2 156.1 156.2 157.3 158.2 161.1 162.3 165.1
171.1 177.1 181.1 182.1 183.1 193.2

From baseline

10.1 12.3 14.1 16.2 17.2 17.3 19.2 23.2 24.1 25.1
26.3 31.3 33.1 33.3 37.1 37.3 39.1 42.2 48.1 49.2
55.2 57.1 60.2 61.1 63.2 64.3 65.1 67.2 69.2 73.1
76.1 76.2 79.2 81.2 85.3 86.2 88.1 89.3 97.3 100.2
102.2 104.1 109.2 109.3 113.1 113.2 114.3 122.1
127.1 127.2 132.2 133.1 133.2 138.1 139.1 151.2
152.1 153.1 166.1 166.2 168.2 168.3 169.2 171.2
176.2 177.2 177.3 181.2 183.2 184.2 185.1 189.3
190.2 191.1 193.3 197.2

NCAA Basketball offense — Plays 2017-2018

From sideline

13.1 35.4 36.2 41.3 55.1 56.3 135.2 149.3 169.4 170.1 196.2

Against

Zone defense

Offense

29.1 53.2 83.3 149.2 195.1

Baseline

18.2 20.2 31.1 44.2 46.1 53.1 63.1 67.3

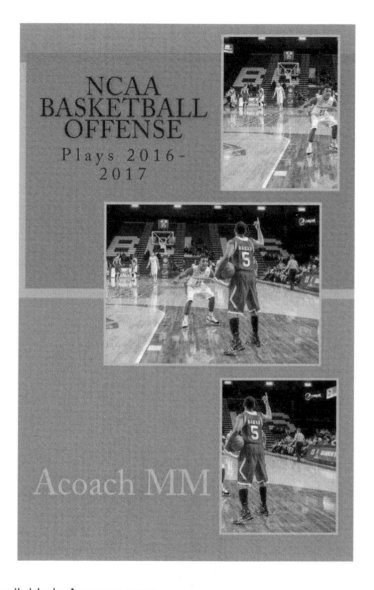

Available in Amazon.com
Only diagrams.
Best teams, best players and best coaches

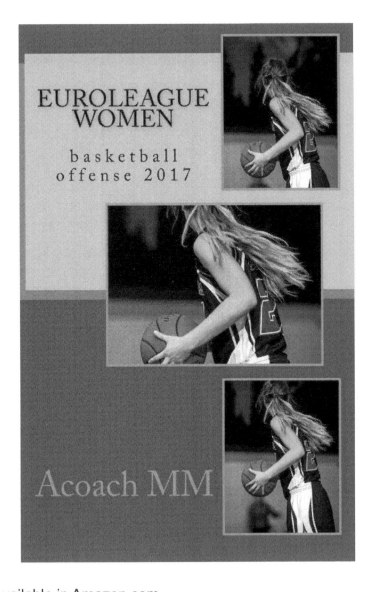

Available in Amazon.com
Only diagrams.
Best teams, best players and best coaches

Other books

Available in Amazon.com
Only diagrams.
Best teams, best players and best coaches

Available in Amazon.com
Only diagrams.
Best teams, best players and best coaches

Made in the USA
San Bernardino, CA
03 March 2018